NEW HOPE FOR THE HUNGRY?

the challenge of the world food crisis

larry minear

Friendship Press • New York

Minear, Larry, 1936-
   New hope for the hungry?

   Bibliography: p.
   1. Famines.   2. Food supply.   3. Food relief.
I. Title.
HC79.F3M56   338.1'9   75-11782
ISBN 0-377-00043-4

Contents

introduction

As I sit down to write this book in January, 1975, half a billion hungry people darken the world. When this book is published in June, 1975, the number may have multiplied or possibly receded a bit. When you read this book sometime thereafter, a harvest or two later, the situation will have changed again.

Why write or read this book if it is out of date before it is set in print? Because the world food crisis is here to stay. It will not be solved by a fine harvest or two, by good rains returning to West Africa, by floods receding from parts of Southern Asia, or by normal growing seasons revisiting the American Midwest. In fact, a few good harvests might create the dangerous illusion that the world food problem has been solved.

The crisis is more than a matter of meteorology, although cooperative weather would surely help. Good rains will not change the fact that about one third of the world's people grow two thirds of the world's food and consume far more than they need. Proper sun will not correct the plight of poorer nations whose food import costs have outrun the values of their exports. Longer growing seasons will not help would-be farmers in developing nations who lack the seeds and tools, the credit and expertise and sometimes even the land itself to take advantage of whatever weather comes along. Meteorology and also agronomy and nutrition help us understand the food crisis, but we also need insights from economics, history, political science and international relations.

I am an expert in few of these fields. My major exposure to the food crisis has been personal rather than academic. My most recent job assignments have involved dealing with U.S. domestic poverty problems, assisting in refugee resettlement in the Southern Sudan and serving as consultant on world hunger to Church World Service and Lutheran World Relief. I represent these two agencies in Washington and the UN and in that capacity attended the recent World Food Conference. My assignments, contacts and colleagues have enriched my understanding of the crisis immeasurably, although the book which follows represents my own perceptions and not necessarily those of others.

Growing out of these professional and personal experiences, *New Hope for the Hungry?* is not a technical treatise on the food crisis. It is not a report on the World Food Conference, although much of its material is drawn from there. Nor is it first and foremost a call for action by UN bodies, governments or citizens. It is an attempt to paint a picture for other generalists of the broad dimensions of the world food problem, augmented by the human details which belong in the foreground. It seeks to answer questions being asked by many concerned persons, inside the churches and out, and to highlight and encourage constructive actions. It lists basic documents and stimulating books for those who wish more detailed information.

I write primarily with American and Canadian audiences in mind, using also illustrative material from other countries. I rely largely on the basic data prepared by the UN for the World Food Conference since it is now accepted by governments as the baseline for discussions of the crisis. I devote considerable space to the efforts of private agencies, primarily churches, because these are of interest to readers and are essential to coping with a crisis which is too important and too urgent to be left to governments.

The title is intended to be interrogatory: *New Hope for the Hungry?* My basic thesis is that if the challenge of the world food crisis is seen for what it is, as a critical test of our technical know-how and our resourcefulness, of our vision and our commitment to each other, then the world community will respond speedily and effectively before the crisis becomes altogether unmanageable. Private citizens, individual nations, and nations-in-concert have become "ominously conscious", as one speaker at the World Food Conference put it, "of the thin edge between hope and hunger." They have begun to take actions which provide new hope for the hungry. But the hope is still embryonic and the future is fraught with possibilities of confrontation and conflict as well as of cooperation and interdependence.

So the question we ask is real and not hypothetical. While it is easier to ask, to write and to read about the needs of the hungry than to satisfy them, this volume is intended to contribute to an affirmative and concrete answer to our basic question. For people of good will, there can be no other answer.

1

the hungry:
who are they?

The hungry are people who don't have enough to eat. They live on every continent and in virtually every country, though more frequently in the southern hemisphere and in developing countries than elsewhere. They are of every race, religion, tribe and tongue, though more frequently than not they are non-white, non-Christian, and non-English speaking. They are underemployed and unemployed, the economically powerless.

Most hungry people live in rural areas, although the urban poor are the more vulnerable to extreme hunger. Most live off the land, which they may or may not own. Most are members of large families in societies of rapidly growing populations. Most are without political power. Many are children, many are women—including pregnant and nursing mothers—and a large number are old.

By generally accepted estimates, their number in the early 1970s was one half billion people. An unknown number who were among the hungry then have since died; their places have been more than filled by others. Still others may shortly join them. The queue already encircles the globe.

The Geography of Hunger

We have adequate information to draw the grim map of hunger. It is based on data submitted by national governments to the UN for analysis and action. We will use it fairly selectively and gingerly, realizing that while some statistics are indispensable, a steady bombardment may produce more shellshock than understanding.

Based on very conservative estimates, one out of every eight persons alive in 1970 was hungry. Of the 3.8 billion people on the planet, 12 percent, or 462 million lacked sufficient food. Almost nineteen out of every twenty of the world's hungry people (434 out of 462 million) lived in developing countries. A child born there had far greater chances of ending up hungry than its counterparts born elsewhere. The situation has gotten even worse since 1970.

Hunger is most densely concentrated in the Far Eastern region, particularly in Southern Asia. Three out of every ten people in that region (301 million) are hungry. In Africa it is one out of four (67 million), in the Near East about 18 percent (30 million), and in Latin America about 13 percent (36 million).

In developed regions, 3 percent (28 million people) are malnourished. Exact figures are not available for the one billion people of China, North Korea, North Vietnam and Mongolia, but malnutrition of a degree about half as serious as in other developing countries is understood to affect 8 to 10 percent (or 80 to 100 million) of their population. This would bring the malnourished population of the world to more than 500 million, or about one in every seven persons on the planet.

Fifty-seven of the 97 "developing countries," to use the UN's categories, lacked sufficient food in the early 1970s for their people. Recent agonies have placed 33 of these and their almost one billion people on the critical list. Members of this group probably add substantially to the ranks of the 462 million people who are chronically malnourished. Their 33 countries are, in the language of the UN, the Most Seriously Affected nations (MSAs) and are listed on Chart 1.

How severe are the food needs of people in the neediest countries and elsewhere in the southern hemisphere? The recommended minimum daily adult calorie consumption in most climates is 3200 calories for men and 2300 for women. Protein intake, depending on its quality and quantity, should be in the daily range of 46-56 grams (about 1.6-2.0 ounces) for adults, about half as much for children. Good nutrition depends on enough calories for energy and enough protein for body building and repair. Extremely inadequate protein intake over extended periods of time leads to kwashiorkor, a condition marked by distended stomachs and swollen limbs. Extremely inadequate total food intake leads to marasmus, a wasting away of body tissues. The average calorie and protein intake of the MSAs and other countries as compared to these recommended minimum daily amounts is shown on Map 1.

On Map 1 the neediest countries are shaded to indicate the hungriest nations of the world. If we

CHART 1

The 33 Most Seriously Affected Countries (MSAs)
(with 1974 populations in millions)

The Far East

Bangladesh (76 million estimated)	
Cambodia	(7)
India	(563)
Laos	(3)
Pakistan	(67)
Sri Lanka	(13)

The Near East

Yemen Arab Republic (North)	(6)
Yemen People's Democratic Republic (South)	(2)

Latin America

El Salvador	(4)
Guyana	(1)
Haiti	(5)
Honduras	(3)

Africa

Central African Republic	(2)
Chad	(4)
Dahomey	(3 est.)
Ethiopia	(27)
Ghana	(9)
Guinea	(4 est.)
Ivory Coast	(5 est.)
Kenya	(12)
Lesotho	(1)
Malagasy Republic	(7)
Mali	(5)
Mauritania	(1 est.)
Niger	(4)
Rwanda	(4)
Senegal	(4 est.)
Sierra Leone	(3)
Somalia Democratic Republic	(3 est.)
Sudan	(17)
Tanzania	(14)
United Republic of Cameroon	(5,6)
Upper Volta	(6 est.)

Information for this chart compiled by the United Nations

drew a map on which the size of each MSA was related to its proportion of the world's total population, we would have a more accurate picture of world hunger, with the United States and Canada drastically diminished in size. Better yet, if our map showed a country's size in proportion to its share of the world's hungry people, the message would be starker still. The United States would then be about the size of Bangladesh, with an area roughly equal to that of the state of Illinois.

Each country, rich or poor, needs its own hunger map. The U.S. map would show a stippled pattern, with the hungry concentrated in urban areas (particularly inner cities), in the more impoverished rural regions (such as Appalachia), on Indian reservations and among migrant workers. According to the 1970 census, the low-income population was composed of 60.5 percent White, 29.5 percent Black, 8.5 percent of Spanish origin, and 1.5 percent Indian and other.

According to U.S. government figures for 1974, roughly 40 million low-income persons were eligible for participation in the U.S. food stamp program. Of these, as of the year's end, about 17 million were enrolled. The 23 million who were not enrolled, since they lacked the money to purchase adequate diets, were probably malnourished. Those enrolled, while more able to cope with their nutritional needs, were not out of nutritional danger due to the difficulties of purchasing adequate diets even with the extra buying power provided by food stamps. Also at nutritional risk were the millions of "near poor" or "working poor," who at the time of a given survey may have adequate income for good nutrition but due to problems of seasonal unemployment or recession may drop below the poverty line at various times during the year. Thus while it is possible to say that 23 million Americans in 1974 were probably malnourished, there is good evidence to suggest (despite some conflicting and incomplete data) that the number who were malnourished at one time or another during the year was considerably higher.

Comparable figures are not available for Canada. The final results of "Nutrition Canada," a survey conducted in 1973 for the Department of National Health and Welfare, are not expected until 1976. Preliminary findings establish only that those Canadians at greatest nutritional risk are the Eskimos, followed by the Indians and in turn by the general population.

The figures for the hungry in the United States and Canada would appear to contradict those of the UN, which estimated that there were 28 million hungry persons in all developed nations combined in 1970. The UN figures were for 1970, while the U.S. figures were for 1972. Also, the UN uses a very conservative definition of hunger while the U.S. figures include along with the chronically malnourished those who are hungry at the end of the month.

Hunger in the United States and other developed countries may seem more real to some because it is a bit nearer at hand; but the geography of hunger needs first and last a world map, whether using a Mercator or a Hunger projection. For hunger is global in nature, as its solutions must be. "History records more acute shortages in individual countries," said the UN in 1974 as it reflected on this data, "but it

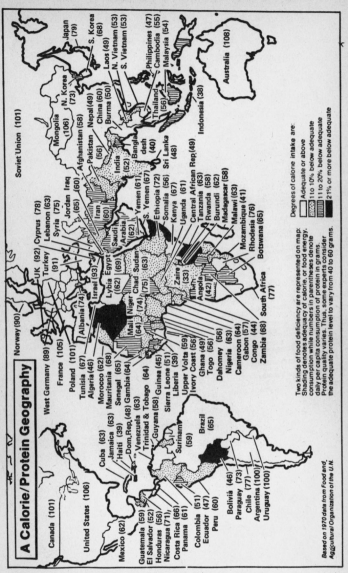

A Calorie/Protein Geography

Canada (101)

United States (106)

Mexico (62)

Guatemala (59)
El Salvador (52)
Honduras (56)
Nicaragua (71)
Costa Rica (66)
Panama (61)

Cuba (63)
Jamaica (63)
Haiti (39)
Dom. Rep. (48)
Venezuela (63)
Trinidad & Tobago (64)
Guyana (58)
Surinam (59)

Colombia (51)
Ecuador (47)
Peru (60)

Bolivia (46)
Paraguay (73)
Chile (77)
Argentina (100)
Uruguay (100)

Brazil (65)

Norway (90)

West Germany (89)
France (105)
Poland (101)
UK (92)
Cyprus (78)
Turkey (75)
Lebanon (63)
Syria (75)
Jordan (65)
Iraq (60)
Israel (93)
Albania (74)
Tunisia (67)
Algeria (46)
Morocco (62)
Mauritania (68)
Senegal (65)
Gambia (64)
Guinea (45)
Sierra Leone (51)
Liberia (39)
Upper Volta (59)
Ivory Coast (56)
Ghana (49)
Togo (56)
Dahomey (56)
Nigeria (63)
Cameroon (64)
Gabon (57)
Congo (44)
Zambia (68)

Soviet Union (101)

Mongolia (106)
Afghanistan (58)
Pakistan (49)
Nepal (49)
China (60)
Burma (50)
India (52)
Bangladesh (40)
Sri Lanka (48)
Iran (60)
Saudi Arabia (62)
Egypt (69)
Lybia (62)
Chad (74)
Niger (64)
Mali (64)
Sudan (63)
Yemen (61)
S. Yemen (67)
Ethiopia (72)
Somalia (56)
Kenya (67)
Uganda (61)
Central African Rep. (49)
Zaire (33)
Angola (42)
Tanzania (63)
Rwanda (58)
Burundi (62)
Malawi (63)
Mozambique (58)
Rhodesia (76)
Botswana (65)
South Africa (77)
Madagascar (76)

N. Korea (73)
Japan (79)
S. Korea (68)
Laos (49)
N. Vietnam (53)
S. Vietnam (53)
Philippines (47)
Cambodia (55)
Malaysia (54)
Thailand (56)

Indonesia (38)

Australia (108)

Two kinds of food deficiency are represented on map:
Shading denotes adequacy of calorie, or food energy,
consumption while numbers in parentheses denote
daily per capita consumption of protein in grams.
Protein quality varies. Thus, some experts consider
the adequate protein level to vary from 40 to 60 grams.

Degrees of calorie intake are:

☐ Adequate or above
☐ 1 to 10% below adequate
☐ 11 to 20% below adequate
■ 21% or more below adequate

*Based on 1970 data from Food and
Agricultural Organization of the U.N.*

Reprinted from *The New York Times* (July 26, 1974). Updated with protein data through 1972 supplied by
the UN World Food Conference Secretariat. © 1974 by The New York Times Company. Reprinted by permission.

Author's Note: Since some persons consume more than others, the national average of protein or calorie
consumption does not mean that there are not many persons either above or below that figure.

is doubtful whether such a critical food situation has
ever been so world-wide."

The Demography of Hunger

What can the demographer, the statistician of
populations, add to this geography of hunger?

First, the hungry are usually the poor, although
there are poor people who are not malnourished and
rich people who are. The main cause of hunger is
poverty, says the UN. Hunger results "from socio-
economic development patterns which in most of the
poorer countries have been characterized by a high
degree of concentration of power, wealth and income
in the hands of relatively small elites of national or
foreign individuals or groups."

Consider the distribution of income and land
among the poor. In many developing countries, the
upper 40 percent of the population receives three
quarters of all the income, leaving the remaining quarter to be shared by 60 percent of the people. The
nearly one billion people in the Most Seriously
Affected of the developing countries have average
annual incomes of less than $400. Most live on less
than thirty cents per day.

As for land, in most poor nations 20 percent of
the landowners own more than half of the land.
In Venezuela, this 20 percent owns 82 percent, in
Brazil 53 percent, in the Philippines, Pakistan and
India, roughly 50 percent. In Ethiopia the picture may
be changing, but until recently 85 percent of the arable
land was owned by the royal family, the feudal aristoc-
racy and the Coptic Church. In developing countries

there are well over 100 million farms of 12.5 acres or less, more than half of them less than 2.5 acres. The average farmer owns only a few acres or is sharecropper on another's land, insecure and beholden. The small subsistence farmers who can feed their families from their own land are somewhat better off than the landless agricultural laborers who are virtually without income except during planting and harvest seasons.

More than 70 percent of the people in poorer countries live in rural areas. Their governments generally spend only a third to a quarter as much per person on them as on those living in cities. The rural poor thus bear the brunt of unevenly distributed government services, technical know-how and equipment as well as capital and credit, land and water. The urban poor, many of them having exchanged rural poverty for urban misery, get an uneven shake in employment opportunities and access to food at affordable prices. With no chance of growing their own food and little chance of earning the money to buy it, the urban poor are even more prone than their rural kinfolk to hunger.

The main distinction among the poor, however, is not that between rural and urban poor people. It is between absolute and relative poverty. "Absolute poverty," says Robert McNamara, president of the World Bank, "is a condition of life so degraded by disease, illiteracy, malnutrition and squalor as to deny its victims basic human necessities. . . . The absolute poor are not merely a tiny minority of unfortunates— a miscellaneous collection of the losers in life—a regrettable but insignificant exception to the rule.

On the contrary, they constitute roughly 40 percent of the nearly two billion individuals living in developing nations." Relative poverty, on the other hand, means simply that "some countries are less affluent than other countries or that some citizens of a given country have less personal abundance than their neighbors."

The chronically hungry, then, are mainly the absolute poor, caught not only without food, but also without basic health, education and employment opportunities. They are, says the UN, the victims of "the extreme inequality in the food distribution between socio-economic groups" within a given country, which, as we shall see, mirrors a similar inequality between rich and poor countries at the international level.

Within poor families, the hungriest people are generally the children, "the first victims" of food shortages; in UNICEF's words. It is not that their parents don't love them. "An inactive child is not as damaging to the family's survival as an inactive adult," says the UN. "If there is not enough food for the whole family, the working adults tend to take for themselves the largest share. This is particularly serious because children and women in pregnancy and lactation have additional nutritional needs." Often the deprivation happens unintentionally, the longer term effects being concealed from parents at the time. The infant mortality rate in developing countries is about ten times what it is elsewhere, with one child in four not reaching age five. One in every two infant deaths in poorer nations is linked to malnutrition.

Sharply declining food supplies in 1974 led UNICEF to declare a World Child Emergency. Of the 1.2 billion children in developing countries, an estimated 210 million are malnourished: 10 million severely, 80 million moderately, and 120 million mildly. Every one of the almost 500 million children living in the hardest hit nations, however, is potentially vulnerable to malnutrition sooner or later, even though some are safe for the time being. Whatever the uncertain future brings, there is now one malnourished child in the world for every American, and the hungry children are increasing faster than the Americans.

The demographer can tell us more. Most of the hungry, viewed from developed countries, would be called members of racial minority groups. But from a global perspective, their racial and ethnic backgrounds form the world's non-white majority: Oriental, Black, Latin-American, Arab and Aborigine. They are Muslims and Hindus, Christians and animists, monotheists, worshippers of tribal deities and of no deity at all. Many are unskilled and without formal education. Most are members of large families, living in remote areas without adequate transportation and communication. Most have been untouched by governmental programs, including "foreign aid."

These socio-economic items suggest some political hypotheses. In many countries, people without land or other assets are without influence. Persons without economic leverage very often lack the power to improve their situation, since economic and political powerlessness frequently go hand in hand. Unlike the situation in the United States, where rural areas have

until recently exercised disproportionate influence at
the national and state levels, the rural areas in many
developing countries are the forgotten places. Yet
since for all of their power, rural politicians in the
United States have seldom been champions of the
rural poor, there is a certain kinship between the
rural poor in the United States and those in Asia,
Africa and Latin America.

This is not to say that governments—whether
socialist, communist or democratic, tribal or imperial,
one party or multi-party—uniformly write off the
hungry. In fact, widespread discontent among hungry
people can have unsettling effects on governments of
any persuasion. In Ethiopia, the failure of the
emperor and his officials to respond to famine conditions was one factor in their ouster in 1974. In that
year, that and other reasons led to the unseating of
the government in Niger, West Africa. The Indian
government was reported in late 1974 to be concentrating its limited food distribution in its swollen
cities where potential hunger riots posed the greatest
peril to its stability. Various countries, for political
as well as social and economic reasons, have tried
schemes to resettle the urban poor back into rural
areas. Politicians take the demography of hunger
into account one way or another in most decision-
making.

So most of the hungry live on the hundred million
small farms in more than a million villages in developing countries. They farm whatever small land they
have access to with traditional implements such as
hoes, axes, pangas. They have very little to help them,

such as schools and clinics, credit unions, cooperatives or agricultural extension agents. They have little
say in their affairs and little apparent power to
change their situation.

The Humanity of the Hungry

Whatever the conclusions of geographers, demographers and other social scientists, the hungry are
first and last human beings. We know some of their
faces, though not many of us see them in a mirror.
We feel we know the eyes, the bellies, the matchstick
frames, the listless spirits, although few of us are
likely to say, "Some of my best friends are hungry."
How many of the world's half billion hungry people

MENE TEKEL ...

Behrendt — Het Parool, Amsterdam   ROTHCO

have we actually met? There is a certain apartness to hunger, here and elsewhere.

The writer of this book, like many of its readers, knows very little about what it feels like to be hungry. When were we ever without food for more than a few hours? If our memories go back to World War II days, we may recall rationing and victory gardens. If we were alive during the 1930s, we may have known some genuinely hard times. But for many of us, our most recent memory of scarcity may have been a temporary shortage of gas—a jolt to be sure, and an inconvenience, but hardly akin to the chronic absence of food. Such inconveniences as we have known—and this is not to minimize the suffering of the genuinely hungry among us—are signs of relative rather than absolute deprivation. "It's necessary to know hunger to know how to describe it," wrote Carolina Maria de Jesus from a malnourished Brazilian slum in 1958. Not knowing hunger, can we really say anything very meaningful about what will provide new hope for the hungry?

Can we really profess to be concerned about the hungry people of Asia, Africa, and Latin America when we seem to care so little about the malnourished people among us? Perhaps hunger at home makes hunger real elsewhere, and until hunger stops being a problem and starts being a person it will continue to be somehow unreal. Do we assume that because there are apparently no bloated bellies in our neighborhood or nation, there is no malnutrition? Can we care about hunger on one side of a political boundary line but not on the other? Here or there, the hungry and we live in two different worlds. As in the Behrendt cartoon, most of us are off the map when it comes to the world of real hunger. We can and must affirm the humanity of the hungry, but for most of us the affirmation is an act of faith rather than a fact of personal experience.

The geographer's and demographer's data, impersonal though it be, calls into question whether the humanity of the hungry may not be undermined by the degrading conditions in which they exist. Can one live a fully human life on 39 grams of protein per day in Haiti? on 30 cents a day in India? on postage-stamp plots in Ethiopia? Can the essential qualities of human life be preserved in absolute poverty, "a condition of life so limited," in the view of the World Bank, "as to prevent realization of the potential of the genes with which one is born; a condition so degrading as to insult human dignity—and yet a condition of life so common as to be the lot of some 40 percent of the peoples of the developing countries?"

Many of us instinctively answer in the affirmative. Yes, the human spirit can triumph over even the most hopeless conditions. Before leaping to any such easy conclusion, however, let us listen to the minister of agriculture of Bangladesh, a nation for whom hunger, he reminds us, is "the burden of daily existence." He warned fellow delegates at the World Food Conference in late 1974 that "starvation and malnutrition are not only eroding the efficiency of the work force in the developing world, but are also leading to a genetic degeneration.

"It may not be far-fetched to imagine that the situation, if allowed to continue long, will end up with two classes of human beings—one affluent, aggressive and authoritarian, the other depressed, servile and degraded. We owe it to ourselves and to our children to prevent such a cataclysmic degeneration of human society."

The Human Impact

Four vignettes enable us better to sense the effects of hunger on human beings. Other illustrations are available elsewhere and, for the fortunate, from personal experience. The first describes hungry people in late 1974 in Bangladesh. Howard Jost, Church World Service representative in Dacca, gave this report to a U.S. Senate hearing on world food needs in December, 1974 when official estimates placed starvation deaths in the previous two months at 27,000. Unofficial estimates were running as high as 100,000.

In the huge crowd of over 5 million severely affected people, it is hard to see individual faces and to understand what all this means to the actual people involved. Because of Bangladesh's large and rapidly growing population, farm sizes have shrunk to two acres on an average and in many, many cases much less. These landless and near-landless must work at other jobs to supplement their income. When the recent floods wiped out the crops nearly ready for harvest, they also wiped out the employment for these people. With no harvest and no work, they have been forced to sell their household belongings, cattle, perhaps their little bit of land as well, in an effort to raise money for food to tide them over the hard times.

They join the swelling ranks of the land wanderers.

Many of them come to the cities looking for work or for food. Usually they find little of either and the process of starvation continues a bit more quickly. Their children, weak already, now crowd the feeding centers which haven't enough food (let alone milk) to feed them. Some roam streets near the shopping areas of the wealthy residential sections of the city begging for food. Others, too weak and dispirited, sit mutely at the side of the road, waiting for passers by to throw them a coin or two. Some women are forced into prostitution, some men into thievery. The rate of suicides has increased (including families who take poison rather than face the hungry days) and so has disease. The cost in terms of impaired mental and physical abilities is enormous, while at the same time money, time and other resources which were intended for development efforts are diverted into relief projects.

The second account was written in early 1974, by Jon Otto, Church World Service representative in Niger, West Africa. He describes one of the individual faces of hunger.

The Sahara winter wind whistled cold and dusty as we squatted in front of the nomad's skin tent at the edge of town. My young Tuareg host seemed not to notice the biting January wind that snapped at his tattered robe. He spoke in plain words of the tragedy his family is suffering, a story often repeated in the drought-stricken West African country of Niger.

Only a few years ago they had been successful cattle herders, living a hard but healthy life on the scrubland his people love. Then for the past five years less and less rain had fallen. Helplessly they watched their animals die of famine and thirst. Finally in desperation he, Sidi Mohamman, and his brother Usseni decided to trek southward away from the desert toward the town of Maradi where they heard food was available.

With meager possessions packed on their remaining
three donkeys and two camels they had begun walking
in early November. There were ten of them when they
left: two brothers, their aging mother, Sidi's wife and
their six children. Thirty-two grueling days later only
nine of them arrived in Maradi. Fatigued and weakened
by a recent pregnancy, Sidi's wife had died en route.

When Sidi rolled back a scrap of blanket to show me
his infant son, it was all I could do to keep from looking
away from the lifeless form. With no mother's milk the
boy had wasted away to skin and bones. Soon there
would be eight of them only. Unable to feed his family
Sidi had tried to give away the two youngest daughters.
Among such poor people no takers were found.

There was no food distribution in Maradi when they
arrived in December. Sidi and Usseni sold the animals
one by one to buy food. The two teenage sons went
into Maradi begging, but competition is stiff these days.
With a normal population of over 30,000, Maradi must
now contend with the influx of thousands of starving
families like Sidi's. They live in improvised huts com-
pletely surrounding the town that is now their only
chance for survival.

For some, death will come more quickly than for
others. Long isolated in outlying areas, these hunger
refugees are being decimated by unfamiliar diseases.
Cholera and measles spread rapidly among people who
have no immunity. Dysentery and hepatitis meet little
resistance in these weakened bodies. . . .

What will come next? Sidi did not seem to hear my
final question as he squinted into the grey-blue winter
sky. Then he methodically repeated what must be the
prayer of his life: If we can survive till the next rainy
season, which surely must come this year, if we can
somehow get together a few animals, if Allah wills, then
we will go home.

Walking back to town across the sandy field an old
struggle raged inside of me. It was profound pessimism
wrestling with renewed dedication. Sidi hasn't got a

chance, one side would say. No, he sure does not if we give up on him, the retort came back. This continuing debate always ends in stalemate. Yet, Sidi and family are out there. If they are giving it their best to make it, or die trying, then who are we to give up?

Ms. Carolina Maria de Jesus lived in a favela, or slum, in Sao Paulo, Brazil with her three children for more than a decade. She was unmarried and unemployed. She managed to scavenge enough food for her family by collecting paper, rags and metal each day from the streets and alleys of the city and selling them to junk dealers. She also found food for her family in garbage pails, at the city dumps and among the discards of markets, slaughterhouses and canning factories. For a number of years she kept a diary which was later published in newspaper and book form in Brazil, earning her money enough to leave the favela behind. Her writing was always candid. "Once every four years," she wrote, "the politicians change without solving the problem of hunger that has its headquarters in the favela and its branch offices in the workers' homes." The following is her diary entry for July 15, 1959.*

> When I got out of bed, Vera [her daughter] was already awake and she asked me:
> "Mama, isn't today my birthday?"
> "It is. My congratulations. I wish you happiness."
> "Are you going to make a cake for me?"
> "I don't know. If I can get some money."

---

*From *Child of the Dark*, The Diary of Carolina Maria de Jesus. Translated by David St. Clair. Copyright © 1962 by E. P. Dutton & Co., Inc., and Souvenir Press, Ltd. Reprinted by permission of the publishers, E. P. Dutton & Co., Inc.

I lit the fire and went to carry water. The women were complaining that the water was running out slow.

The garbagemen have gone by. I got little paper. I went by the factory to pick up some rags. I began to feel dizzy. I made up my mind to go to Dona Angelina's house to ask for a little coffee. Dona Angelina gave me some. When I went out I told her I was feeling better.

"It's hunger. You need to eat."

"But what I earn isn't enough."

I have lost eight kilos. I have no meat on my bones, and the little I did have has gone. I picked up the papers and went out. When I went past a shop window I saw my reflection. I looked the other way because I thought I was seeing a ghost.

"Mommy, how come they can't pay us for not eating what they pay the farmers not to grow?"

Uluschak—Edmonton Journal, Canada   ROTHCO

I fried fish and made some corn mush for the children to eat with the fish. When Vera showed up and saw the mush inside the pot she asked:

"Is that a cake? Today is my birthday!"

"No it isn't cake. It's mush."

"I don't like mush!"

I got some milk. I gave her milk and mush. She ate it, sobbing.

Who am I to make a cake?

Ms. Barbara Jones (a real person, with a fictitious name) lives in Baltimore, Maryland with her four children. She is 27 years old. In late 1974, she and her family were among the 17 million participants in the $4 billion-a-year federal food stamp program. Each month she received a check of $198 from the State Welfare Department. From it she paid $125 for rent and $25 for utilities, leaving $48 for food and other essentials.

She was entitled to buy $178 in food stamps for $60, but she did not have $60. Instead, she spent $30 and got $89 worth of stamps. Later each month she received a support payment from her former husband of $38.80, with which she sometimes purchased additional food stamps. But the checks were not always on time and there were often delays in issuing the stamps. While her family generally had nutritious meals early in the month, they were often hungry later on.

If Ms. Jones had been able to spend the full $60 for food stamps, she would have had about 40 cents per person per meal. Using the "Economy Diet Plan" prepared by the U.S. Department of Agriculture, she might have been able to prepare adequate meals for

her family (although many question the adequacy of
diets possible under this plan and at this price). However, with neither enough money nor food, the nutritional balance of the family diet suffered. Occasionally
she was forced to choose between food and utilities.

These four vignettes provide a glimpse of the
human side of hunger. The human dimension must
not be obscured as we now turn to the causes of the
suffering of half a billion persons and then to some
possible remedies.

2

the causes

World hunger has taken many people, including the experts, by surprise. Although the world didn't simply wake up one morning and discover the existence of half a billion hungry people, few persons saw a disaster of such monumental proportions in the making. The crisis has been with us long enough now to enable us to sort out why it happened. Today's devastating food shortages were triggered by several recent events. These events at the same time disclosed some more fundamental problems.

Recent Events

World food scarcity is quite new to the 1970s. The late 1960s had been good years for agriculture throughout the world. Grain production was up, more than outdistancing population in both developing and developed countries. New high-yielding varieties of grains were coming into their own. India, staggered by drought in the mid sixties, built up her grain reserves to almost ten million tons by the decade's end. North America had enormous surpluses, some piled high in town streets after grain elevators were full. But then the picture changed.

In 1971, bad weather slashed harvests in many developing countries, and in 1972 developed countries were affected as well. World grain production in 1972 was down for the first time since World War II. In 1973, weather was better, but no developing region recovered fully and some, like West Africa, continued to slip.

The year 1974 began promisingly, but by autumn the drought in the U.S. and the uneven monsoons in Asia had taken a heavy toll. By early 1975, India, its grain reserves long since exhausted, had purchased seven million tons of grain abroad and was seeking an additional half million. From a global viewpoint, a UN official summed it all up. "The period of [food] insecurity and instability will now be further prolonged. . . . Humanity must continue to live from hand to mouth for another season or two at least, with the grave danger of starvation that this entails for the world's poor."

Other factors joined the freaky weather to help create a hungrier world. Scarce food was sought after by nations with poor harvests. Russia alone tripled its imports of grain in 1972/73 to 30 million tons, much of it from the U.S. The prices of U.S. wheat and soybeans for export rose four-fold, corn three-fold, between 1972 and 1974. The grain import costs of poor countries tripled in three years. India paid to U.S. suppliers in late 1974 alone $400 million more than the same grain would have cost a year earlier. And, like Ms. Jones' family in Chapter 1, forced by mounting food prices to eat less and buy food with funds budgeted for other necessities, India bought food probably with scarce foreign reserves, perhaps (although not certainly) even trimming essential imports like fertilizer and spare parts. Developed nations were slow to provide the neediest countries enough food or food stamps to make ends meet.

In fact, at the time of rising food demand, the U.S., the great breadbasket, grain silo, and food super-market of the world, was sharply reducing surplus stocks and retiring cropland under production. Reserve stocks in various exporting countries were sold off, reducing world grain reserves from 69 days' supply in 1970 to only 26 days' in 1974. The world's food supply came to depend, as now, on the next harvests.

Still other factors made for food shortages. During food crises before the 1970s, massive tonnages of grain had gone from breadbasket countries to areas of human need. Developing countries during the 1960s relied on food aid for more than one third of their total food imports. However, with greater commercial demand and higher grain prices, food aid programs dwindled. World food aid dropped from an average of about 15 million tons annually in the six-ties to less than ten million tons in 1972-73 to only 7.5 million tons in 1973-74. One million tons of grain can feed five million people for a year.

Sharp rises in petroleum prices in 1973/74 made farming in rich and poor countries more expensive. Agriculture which depended on tractors, wells, and pumps felt a direct shock. Shortly the cost of related products such as chemical fertilizers and pesticides, which had been on the way up anyway, were hit as well. Fertilizer not only cost more, but was harder to find since 25 million acres of U.S. lands earlier taken out of production were being re-cultivated. Customers in developed countries out-bid other buyers. The one million tons of fertilizer India was unable to purchase in 1974 would have grown about ten million tons of food and provided subsistence diets for fifty million Indians. Lacking the fertilizer, India then needed to purchase the food, at new high prices, and pay the ocean freight, which had tripled in three years. The gains of the Green Revolution were undercut as its oil-based ingredients became unavailable at reasonable prices. While Americans lined up at gas stations to fill automobile tanks, Indians lined up in longer queues for a few gallons to keep their irrigation pumps and tractors going.

Developing countries in 1974 alone paid an estimated $8-10 billion extra for energy, roughly a tripling in three years, and an additional $5 billion for such food and fertilizer as they could buy. Total foreign aid from all countries to developing nations in 1973, by comparison, was only $9.4 billion. Those countries least dependent on imported food and fuel have suffered least from the shocks of the 1970s. Those which have had to import either food or fuel have been heavily affected. And those needing both food and fuel have experienced double trouble. Many of the latter earn their status as Most Seriously Affected nations in this fashion.

So the early 1970s saw the prices of oil chasing food and fertilizer up the spiral staircase called inflation. There is, to be sure, some dispute as to who was chasing whom, but food and fertilizer had started the race before being joined by oil, after which they both ran faster. There is no question, however, that the staircase was set in a global landscape wracked by drought and uneven monsoons and that the real losers in every country were the poor.

Deeper Roots

This review of recent events raises more questions than it answers. It describes what happened rather than explaining why. If we stopped here, we would be like the doctor who diagnoses a cancer patient's fever as caused by the seventy-two hour flu.

Erratic weather didn't create world hunger. Even in the worst month, the world had enough food for everybody—but there was still widespread starvation. Even when food was scarcest and demand greatest, there was always enough so that children should not have gone to bed hungry. Even higher prices for food, fertilizer, and fuel don't get to the root of the matter. The world is rich enough in money and natural resources to pay the bill. These recent events have surely made things worse. But why have things gotten worse so unevenly? Why have poor people, particularly those in the million villages dotting the southern hemisphere, been the hardest hit?

To answer these questions, one needs to review more than "recent events." Will starting in the 1970s and discussing the weather and supply-and-demand explain why 30 percent of the world's people grow more than 60 percent of the world's food or, conversely, why 70 percent of the world's people grow only 40 percent of the world's food? Can a brief five-year look reveal why one third of the world's population eats three fourths of the world's protein? These are clearly not recent happenings but global patterns with roots in decades and even centuries of history.

The global imbalances behind the food crisis have four major dimensions. These are (1) agricultural productivity, (2) population growth, (3) consumption patterns, and (4) economic relationships. Each shows a lopsidedness between rich and poor nations. Each relates to and reinforces the others. Each is manageable only in relation to the others and only by basic changes in how the world is organized and operates.

(1) Chart 2 takes a twenty-year look at food growing. Rich and poor countries alike managed to grow about 3.1 percent more food each year during the 1950s and 2.7 percent more during the 1960s. This was quite an accomplishment, but not as good as it sounds.

For one thing, the figures for developing countries average bad years against good and regions which did well (like Latin America and the Near East) against others which did not (like Africa). They average countries like China, Thailand, and Lebanon, which broke the 5 percent production mark, against Indonesia, Chad, and Haiti which averaged only 2 percent or below. Secondly, the rich countries in the 1960s were trying to grow *less* food while the poor countries were trying to grow *more*, and the poor nations had less to work with from the start. By growing less food in the last decade than in the previous one, the rich countries succeeded in their objectives, the poor failed. And finally, the population column includes 34 poor countries in which population outdistanced food production for the 20 year stretch.

Why didn't poor countries grow more food? While they are rich in land (with 70 percent of the world's arable surface) and people (many of them under-utilized), their would-be farmers lack much of the know-how, credit, fertilizer and experience to do the job. Many are frustrated by difficulties of rural life, archaic patterns of land distribution and use and inadequacies of government. Many could grow more per acre than they are now doing, although some (for example in Taiwan) already get better yields per acre than do rich-country farmers. India and the U.S. have about the same amount of cropland. If their yields were equal, Indian harvests would more than double.

It is stunning irony, as the Irish minister of agriculture pointed out to the World Food Conference, that "it is precisely those countries which have the greatest numbers and highest proportions of their population engaged in agriculture which are suffering most from hunger and malnutrition"—and, by implication, growing the least food. In Tanzania, for example, 95 percent of the people are engaged in agriculture, and that nation has serious food deficits; in the U.S., less than 5 percent are farmers, and the U.S. grows enough food for massive exports. The latest fertilizer and fuel shortages have simply compounded an already unequal food production situation.

What poor countries lack, rich countries have in abundance, including capital, technology, research, training and experience. Developed countries have

CHART 2

Growth Rates of Food Production and Population
(Average Annual Growth, in Percent)

	1952-62			1962-72		
	Rate of Population Increase	Rate of Food Production Increase		Rate of Population Increase	Rate of Food Production Increase	
		Total %	% per person		Total %	% per person
Developed Countries	1.3	3.1	1.8	1.0	2.7	1.7
Developing Countries	2.4	3.1	0.7	2.4	2.7	0.3
World	2.0	3.1	1.1	1.9	2.7	0.8

Reprinted from the World Food Conference Secretariat's "Assessment of the World Food Situation," p. 30.

massive funds invested in agriculture; farming is a big business, with shares bought and sold on the stock market. They use 75 percent of the world's chemical fertilizer and 85 percent of its pesticides on only 30 percent of the world's arable land. They consume 95 percent of the world's petroleum, some for agricultural machinery, roughly three-quarters of which machinery is in developed countries. Eighty percent of all agricultural research funds are spent in developed countries, 30 percent in North America alone. That leaves only 20 percent for research on the soil, water resources and climate of developing countries. "The least scientifically advanced countries . . . are spending the least on research and need it most," says the UN.

Developed country-style farming, however, has its drawbacks. It tends to be wasteful of energy. The cost of producing one calorie of food energy, according to a recent study in the United States, was 9 calories of fuel energy. The amount of fertilizer needed to produce more food in the overfertilized soils of developed countries is now much higher than elsewhere. Mechanized farming on large acreages may produce more food, but if all the world farmed like the U.S., the world's known petroleum reserves would last less than 30 years. The Chinese therefore rightly ask whether the world can afford a U.S. It is clear that the agricultural system of the wealthy countries (and also of some poorer nations where it has been tried) epitomizes the global imbalance whereby the rich grow more food than the poor and enrich themselves further in the process.

To meet their food needs, developing countries need to grow 3.5-4.0 percent more food each year. Where a farmer grew 1000 pounds of rice last year, he should grow 1040 pounds this year, 1080 next year and so on. What if he does only as well as in the 1960s, growing increments of 27 pounds more each year? If poor countries do only as well as in the last decade, they will by 1985 be short about 85 million tons of grain *each year* in "good" years, or up to 120 million tons in "bad" years. At today's prices, 85 million tons would cost $16 to $18 billion, far more than the investment required to increase local food production by the needed amount. In the unlikely event that the funds could be found, the ships to transport the food could not. And if the weather in 1985 were like that of 1974, would the food itself be availabe at any price?

So the agenda for developing countries during the next decade is clear. Only more locally grown food can reverse their dependence on others for their daily bread. Massive infusions of food undercut not only the solvency but also the dignity of nations like India or individuals like Ms. Jones who are on the receiving end over an extended period of time. Massive food imports inflate the power, for ill as well as good, of those who export it. That power is already so great that poor countries can only grow more food with sizeable help from those nations to whom they are losing the food production race.

(2) The imbalance in population growth between rich and poor nations is also evident from Chart 2. Population is growing fastest where food production

growth is slowest, and vice versa. The people are in one place, the food elsewhere and their presence in such numbers renders two decades of food production gains negligible. What good is three tenths of 1 percent more food (roughly an extra pound or two) each year to a chronically malnourished African who doesn't have the money to pay for it anyway? The data appears to confirm the view of those who think that if developing countries can't grow more food, the least they could do is to produce fewer children. The rich get richer, it seems, while the poor get children.

No one, least of all the developing countries, doubts that population is giving food production a run for its money. The world's population is growing at the rate of 200,000 persons per day. A 2 percent growth rate on Chart 2 represents a doubling of population every 35 years. Few doubt that there are immediate steps which could usefully be taken to slow the pace or that more adequate family planning policies are an essential ingredient in solving the world food crisis. In Bangladesh, with one of the highest birth rates, contraceptives were so scarce in late 1974 that they were selling on the black market. Conversely, however, the evidence does not suggest that the earth is reaching its population limits or that the world food crisis is likely to be solved through universally available contraceptives alone.

The population conundrum is rooted deeply in the fabric of reasons why people have children. Large families serve a variety of deeply felt needs. Multiple breadwinners may be an asset. Children provide a

kind of social security in countries whose governments provide little to senior citizens. Male off-
spring carry forward the family traditions. High
infant mortality lead parents to have many children
so that a few will survive. The reasons are numerous.

Countries with stabilized birth rates appear to be
those effectively meeting the basic human needs of
the broad masses of their populations for food, shelter, health care (including family planning services),
employment and improved roles for women. More
food and other improvements in the quality of life
seem generally in the long run to lead to declining
birth rates. Plows as well as pills have a role to play.
And for the immediate future in the Most Seriously
Affected nations, emergency food aid needs to pre-
cede both plows and pills. A cartoon in Chapter 6
speaks to the point.

There are those who say that food production has
already lost the race to population, or will shortly do
so. Malthus theorized that population was bound to
outrun food production, the former increasing geo-
metrically while the latter grows arithmetically. More
recently, advocates of Triage, the sorting out of
hungry people or nations into those who can be saved
and those who should be written off, have even ques-
tioned the wisdom of relief efforts to keep all who
are hungry alive. Some are suggesting the adoption of
a "lifeboat ethic" wherein the rich within the boat do
not reach out to help the poor outside for fear that
all will sink. Those for whom there is no food should
be allowed to die, so the arguments go, then the track
can be cleared and the race restarted.

But are these correct readings of the situation? There is enough food to go around, and there will continue to be at least through 1985, provided food production targets are met. While concern about population growth cannot wait until 1985, which is just around the corner anyway, consigning the hungry to death between now and then reinforces the problem rather than solves it. There are not too many people for too little food; rather, available food is unevenly distributed. The number of people presents a problem, to be sure; but the more critical problem is that of food distribution. The most widely accepted strategy, therefore, seems to be to improve the quality of life for all, decisively and in the next ten years, to enable population growth to level off accordingly. Refusing to upgrade living standards when the resources to do so exist calls into question not only our priorities but also our ethics and our political will.

(3) What accounts for the lopsided patterns of global food consumption? The facts for the early 1970s as compiled by the UN and other sources are these:

• Developed countries, with 30 percent of the world's population, consume 51 percent of the world's cereal grain. Adding protein in non-cereal forms, the developed countries consume about three-quarters of the world's protein.

• Developed countries feed 370 million tons of grain annually to livestock, more grain than is eaten annually by all the people of India and China combined. More than 90 percent of the U.S. corn, sorghum and (after the oil has been removed) soy crops are fed to livestock. Almost half of the world's fish catch is fed to livestock and pets.

● In developing countries the average annual consumption of cereal grains per person is about 500 pounds, almost all of it in the form of grain. In developed countries, the average is over 1760 pounds, with only 200 pounds consumed directly. The average is lower for India (400 pounds), higher for the U.S. (almost one ton). One American consumes about as much grain in one form or another as five Indians do.

● Indirect grain consumption takes place in such forms as beef (one pound of which takes roughly 8 to 10 pounds of grain to produce), pork (a 1:4 ratio), chicken (1:2), dairy products and grain-based alcoholic beverages. A reduction of U.S. meat consumption by 10 percent per person would, if properly managed, free up an estimated 12 million tons of grain.

● World grain demand is rising by about 30 million tons annually, which is roughly the annual wheat crop of Canada, Argentina, and Australia combined. Twenty-two million tons go each year to the world's 70 million new mouths, 85 percent of them in developing countries. Eight million tons allow the planet's oldtimers to eat "better," as they have done progressively since World War II. World grain production is now at about 1200 million tons per year.

What conclusions may be drawn from these facts? The major one is that unequal consumption patterns are rooted not only in unequal food production patterns but in wide disparities of income. The fact that developed countries produce more food than developing countries is dangerous but not necessarily disastrous; it becomes so when disparities of income are added which prevent the poor countries, and the poor in rich countries, from buying the food they need. In the international and national market-places, food is a commodity, not a human right. Poverty and hunger are cut from the same cloth. Yet there need be no malnutrition anywhere in the world if available food is distributed more equitably, as one sees by dividing 1200 million tons by 3.8 billion people.

Secondly, the world's food supplies are threatened by the appetites of the rich as well as by the fertility of the poor. The baby born in New York or Ottawa is a greater drain on world food and other resources than the child born in Sao Paolo or Jakarta. The United States, with 6 percent of the world's population, consumes about 35 percent of its natural resources. People in developing countries who are living higher and higher off the hog, whether it be a North American, Western European, or Eastern European hog, contribute to the food consumption imbalances at the global level.

Finally, and as a footnote to consumption patterns throughout the world, outright waste is a significant factor. In developing countries, post-harvest losses and spoilage range as high as 40 percent for some of the more perishable crops, while intestinal and other preventable diseases keep human beings from getting the full benefit of the food they do manage to eat. Developed countries, on their side, are notable for what the UN calls "the high amount of food wasted at home or in public eating places." Many people in developed countries suffer from "nutritional diseases of abundance" such as obesity and heart disease. The wiser utilization of food and the reduction of waste everywhere would make existing food go farther, though probably not altering the fundamental imbalances of food consumption at the global level.

(4) World hunger is rooted in basic economic imbalances among nations. Here the twenty-year span of Chart 2 is only the most recent chapter in a longer history. Centuries ago many developing countries were self-sufficient in food. Some had rich agricultural civilizations which boasted careful land use, irrigation and hydraulics, equitable food distribution and sometimes even food reserves. As these nations became colonial possessions, their traditional agricultural patterns changed. Food production was left to subsistence farmers while top priority was given to producing raw materials for export to industries in the northern hemisphere. The people thus suffered double jeopardy. Local food crops became less plentiful and reliable while raw material earnings from colonial buyers seldom reached reasonable levels.

The deputy prime minister of Cuba painted the broader picture for the World Food Conference delegates, an interpretation shared by many other nations as well.

Colonialism first, and economic imperialism later, disrupted those social mechanisms [of earlier agricultural life] but not to introduce European progress nor . . . the advantages of North America's economic growth. They turned those countries into suppliers of raw materials, ransacked their natural resources, imposed oppressive regimes on them and used these for their own profit, severed cultural progress and sentenced the peoples to illiteracy and perpetual backwardness. Their forests were decimated causing the erosion of their lands. Therefore, it is not a historical accident that the indexes of yield per hectare in the countries of Africa and Asia are incomparably lower than the European or North American average, and that the peoples who have conquered their independence in the last decades have had to start from subhuman levels of culture and technology and today lack the essential resources for accomplishing a true leap into development.

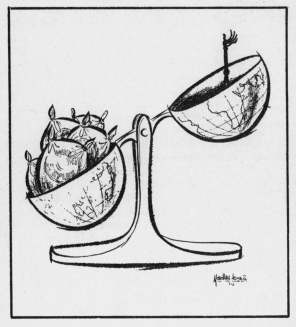

Yardley Jones — Toronto Telegram, Canada　　　**ROTHCO**

The matter is brought more directly into the present by the minister of agriculture of Tanzania, one of the Most Seriously Affected countries and one in which, as we have said, 95 percent of the people live in rural areas and depend on agriculture.

> Through colonialism and imperialism, the world economic order has been operating and is continuing to operate in favor of the "haves" and against the "have-nots." . . . We in Tanzania, through hard effort of our people and progressive socialist economic policies, have achieved tremendous volume increases in all our major crops, but poor prices of these raw materials in world commodity markets, compounded by higher prices of imports from developed countries, have been a major constraint to our efforts to create a self-sustaining economy for the development of our people.
>
> The world food crisis, although triggered off by successive years of drought in many parts of the world, is basically a consequence of the prevailing unjust economic system which leaves inadequate reserves for investment in food production within the Third World Countries. We believe remedial measures to solve the food crisis must include complete international economic readjustment leading to a change of direction in the terms of trade so that they begin, for once, to operate in favour of the developing countries which are now being exploited by the 'Developed' World to the point of poverty, malnutrition, hunger and starvation.

The economic dependence of poor nations on rich nations has not abated substantially with the coming of political independence. The events of the 1970s have simply teamed up with the "agricultural backwardness in two thirds of our planet," in the words of the Cuban delegate, to "turn Nature's accidents into catastrophes." The prices received by poor countries for their exports have been outdistanced by sky-rocketing food import costs.

Developing countries with exports like wool, sisal, cocoa, cotton, and rubber did make some gains in the early 1970s, but those with tea, jute, bananas and lemons to sell did not. In the past two years, Bangladesh has received only 10-15 percent increases in the price of jute, its major export, while the prices of its major imports have jumped three-fold for grain, four-fold for oil and fertilizer, and five-fold for agricultural machinery. Many other developing countries have lost out as well. These trade factors have worsened hunger rather than eased it. They have not, as we shall see in Chapter 4, been offset by outside aid.

In short, these four interlocking imbalances have the hungry world tightly in their grip. Food production is increasing fastest where it is needed least, draining the world's resources disproportionately in the process. Population is expanding fastest in areas of least food supply, precisely where food is needed most. These trends are reinforced by lopsided patterns of consumption and trade among nations and by inequities of social and economic systems within nations. They are not righted by food aid or development assistance. Joined by the recent events reviewed earlier, they have made hunger a world-wide reality.

Projecting these trends into the future, experts agree that without basic shifts in each and every imbalance, today's 500 million chronically malnourished people will by 1985 have become 750 million. Rural populations will have swollen and rural workers increased by 200 million, to say nothing of those who will have migrated to the cities. Barring decisive action to change the trends, which is the subject of the remainder of this book, the UN concludes that "it seems unlikely that the quantity of food per rural inhabitant would be greater in 1985 than it is today . . . and [certainly not enough] to make a significant impact on the general problem of rural poverty and hunger."

The Human Impact

It may seem like a long way from these global imbalances and high sounding analyses of supply and demand to the millions of hungry people around the world. Even the UN statisticians who prepared and analyzed this data, and the World Food Conference which acted on it, had trouble keeping hungry people clearly in view. But each global imbalance has human repercussions. Every percentage point of commercial demand is a jolt for those whose needs are not backed up by money to buy food; and every fraction of a percentage drop in food grown tightens already tight belts even further.

While demographers, economists, and other technicians talk of "imbalances," some may prefer to speak instead of "injustices." For what if not unjust is a world in which the many who produce insufficient food are denied the inputs to produce more? What if not inequitable is a world in which the wealthier nations ride the population escalator down while the poorer countries struggle down the up escalator? What if not a denial of basic equity is a world in which people in some countries feed to livestock and pets and garbage pails enough food to sustain *human* life else-where? And what if not unethical is the world trade game which any number can play, provided the new-comers accept the old stacked deck? Can a world be just in which the malnourished always start from well behind the starting line and then are faulted for not holding their own?

Whether one speaks of imbalances or injustices, the results are the same. Each casualty has a human face. The agony of the millions in Bangladesh is as directly related to underdevelopment and trade in-equities as to floods and war. The tragedy of Sidi and other Tuareg nomads in the Sahel is linked not only to seven years of drought but to centuries of colonial depredation. Ms. de Jesus' hand-to-mouth existence in an urban slum takes place in a country with vast un-tapped agricultural resources and vast non-food exports to developed countries. Ms. Jones' difficulties in warding off malnutrition with food stamps has nothing to do with a national shortage of food. She is a captive of inflated food prices and of a poverty which her country has done scandalously little to alleviate. She is treated by the U.S. much the way many rich countries treat poor countries.

And so, after all the recent events and their deeper roots are analyzed, the human impact remains. That impact is already devastating. What it will become in ten years without decisive action to adjust the under-lying imbalances is unthinkable.

3

the conference

The year 1974 was marked by extraordinary attempts by the international community to come to terms with a hungry and unevenly developed world.

In April, a Special Session of the UN General Assembly on Raw Materials and Development resolved to launch a new international economic order with new rules of the game for developed and developing countries. In August, the World Population Conference in Bucharest reached broad agreement among nations on a world plan of action on population. And in November, the World Food Conference in Rome agreed on measures to deal with the world food crisis.

The World Food Conference was called by the UN in response to requests in 1973 from developing nations and from the United States, all alarmed by the deteriorating world food situation. The Conference served as a giant loom on which governments began to weave a world food policy rug. Weavers from more than 130 of 138 nations were there, assisted by myriad UN agencies and non-governmental organizations. For threads, they used the resources and needs of each country, different in color and texture, in thickness and length. The variegated pattern which emerged sought to be faithful to the many complexities of food production, some of which are noted on Chart 3.

The twenty-three resolutions woven into the new rug range from measures to control African animal trypanosomiasis to the establishment of world food reserves, from the micro to the macro, from the immediate to the longterm. While the rug is far from finished, needing more time, effort and threads, the outlines are clear and correct. Despite minor flaws in some of the workmanship, the creation as a whole offers, in the words of the Pakistani delegate, "a new era of hope for the hungry" in very significant ways.

A Strategy for Integrated Rural Development

In the first place, the world community at the highest levels now agrees on a common assessment of the food crisis, which is a breakthrough, given widely divergent viewpoints on the causes and extent of hunger and malnutrition. Hunger is now the concern of presidents, secretaries of state, and UN secretaries general and no longer a technical matter left to ministers of agriculture. Private citizens, too, have looked beyond the distress of individual countries like Bangladesh to the larger world food crisis in which all lands are caught up. The food crisis has become a political issue in the positive sense that its solutions now require decisions of public policy at the highest levels.

Having recognized the global dimensions of the problem, government delegates accepted its solution as a shared responsibility of the international community. In their words, "the removal of the scourge of hunger and malnutrition, which at present afflicts many millions of human beings, [has become] the objective of the international community as a whole." All nations have now accepted the goal that "within a decade no child will go to bed hungry, that no family will fear for its next day's bread, and that no human being's future and capacities will be stunted by malnutrition."

How will this be achieved? Principally, through integrated rural development in developing countries. What is needed is a set of basic changes in their social and economic fabric to enable production of more food, more equitable distribution and consumption patterns and the improved quality of rural life generally. These changes are "integrated" in the sense that constraints are attacked in a concerted and interdisciplinary fashion by programs to improve medical and educational services, upgrade women's roles, enhance job opportunities and broaden land ownership. The goal is to fulfill basic human needs and potentialities, not simply to make a person a better food grower. It is to be reached by the involvement and mobilization of the people themselves, particularly small farmers and landless laborers, in the shaping of their own lives and institutions. The lasting solution to the world food crisis, the handle for grappling with absolute poverty, is more than food; it is development.

Integrated rural development is primarily the responsibility of developing countries themselves, a responsibility which they accepted fully at the Conference. Each country, poor as well as rich, must see that its own people are fed; while a nation may turn to others for help, the ultimate responsibility resides at home. Developing countries realized that only they can give higher priority to their own agricultural development. Only they can weed out inefficiency and corruption where it exists. Only they can change the way rural economies oppress the poor. "How could the producers of food be expected to feed the hungry when they are themselves oppressed by a life of misery, poverty and deprivation?" asked the delegate from Pakistan. Citing his own country's progress in recent years, the Liberian representative observed that unless the rural farmer is enabled to raise himself "from the mat to the mattress," he will not produce beyond his own needs or contribute to the economic development of his own country.

Integrated rural development, however, is not something that poorer countries can achieve singlehandedly. Richer nations at the Conference acknowledged that only from them can come the financial, technical and material assistance needed to raise food production in poorer countries. Only they can encourage poor countries to produce more by refraining from using their food surpluses in ways which depress agriculture in poor countries. Only they can open their markets to agricultural and raw material exports from Asia, Africa and Latin America at reasonable prices. A number of nations, including the Federal Republic of Germany, Ireland, the Netherlands, Saudi Arabia and the United States made specific pledges toward

CHART 3

Complex Interactions in Food Production

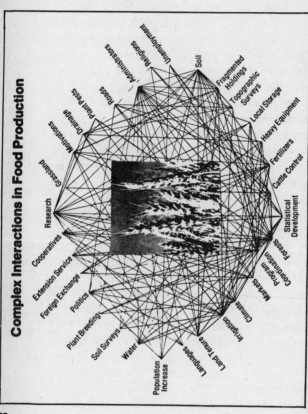

Soil
Fragmented Holdings
Topographic Surveys
Local Storage
Heavy Equipment
Fertilizers
Cattle Control
Statistical Development
Forests
Program Coordination
Markets
Climate
Irrigation
Land Tenure
Languages
Water
Soil Surveys
Population Increase
Plant Breeding
Politics
Foreign Exchange
Extension Service
Cooperatives
Research
Grassland
Motivations
Drainage
Plant Pests
Roads
Administrators
Religions
Unemployment

This chart is based on studies by the Ford Foundation of food production in India, and shows about half of the factors involved in growing more food. It appeared in *The New York Times* on August 10, 1974. © 1974 by The New York Times Company. Reprinted by permission.

the annual $3.5 billion needed from outside sources for investment in agricultural development in poorer countries. Some have also answered the World Bank's request for more funds for agricultural development loans. The Conference also agreed to set up a new International Fund for Agricultural Development.

The UN also has a role within this careful division of labor in the service of integrated rural development. It is to match the needs of poorer countries against the resources of wealthier ones, making sure that the Most Seriously Affected nations are not forgotten. It is to assist with food production, food aid, food security, research and training. Through the World Food Council established by the Conference, the UN can oversee and coordinate the task of completing the weaving of the rug.

To what extent does all of this provide new hope for the hungry? Governments at Rome agreed on promising measures which, if followed up with the swift and specific actions to be described shortly, may reverse the ominous trends described in the previous chapter. They are clearly steps in the right direction, although the goal is far in the distance. "At long last," notes an experienced observer, "we have articulated, as a community of nations, the fundamental priority of agriculture and the needs of the peasant farmer and his family."

An Improved System of Global Food Security

The Conference also took some hopeful steps towards the establishment of a system of world food security. It will have three basic features: (1) an early warning network, (2) world food reserves, and (3) internationally available food aid.

(1) An early warning system has been launched to monitor world food supply-and-demand and weather. It will be based on data supplied by each nation, though China, fearing the abuse of the data, is reluctant to participate. The system will make situations like the West African drought easier to anticipate, although no nation is compelled to act on the warnings provided. Japan will pay the start-up costs of the venture.

(2) World food reserves have been agreed upon to keep the world's cupboard from becoming bare, a grave danger since a major crop failure in one breadbasket country in 1975 could lead quickly to sizeable food shortages elsewhere. Developed and developing countries (again probably without China) will seek to build their own reserves along certain predetermined lines. Together, these will form an international network of national reserves, to be drawn upon by mutual agreement in lean years and replenished in fat years. They will function as something of a shock absorber to offset fluctuations in world food production and prices. The individual reserves themselves will remain under the management and control of each country rather than under international auspices. This is a disappointment to many who fear "food blackmail" and who therefore believe that decisions about who shall be fed and who shall go hungry belong outside the control of individual grain-exporting nations. For the United States, barring new legislation, these reserves will be held by private grain companies, five

of which control 90 percent of U.S. grain exports.

Given the widespread food demand predicted for the next year or two, many national cupboards will not be restocked immediately. Would a country dare build up its food supplies with other nations suffering now? Whether the system becomes fully operational in 1976 or 1980, however, the groundwork has been laid for national larders which together will be better able to cope with world food needs. This will not feed today's hungry but it holds considerable promise for their children tomorrow.

(3) Until poor countries are more self-sufficient and food reserves more generally available, food aid is a matter of life and death for millions of hungry people.

In the 20 years of its Food for Peace Program (Public Law 480), the United States has shipped millions of tons of food overseas. Most of it has been sold to developing countries under Title I of the law at cut-rate prices or on credit. Many nations then resell it through their own commercial channels, using the cash received for governmental programs of various sorts, including military ones. The balance of the food has gone to the UN World Food Program and U.S. voluntary agencies for humanitarian programs under Title II. About 85 percent of all food aid in the past decade has been contributed by the United States. Food aid is also provided by members of the European Economic Community, Canada, Australia, New Zealand, Argentina, and some countries of Eastern Europe.

PL 480 was created when the U.S. had large

unsold and unsellable food surpluses. Now that those
surpluses are gone, food aid has dwindled and food
aid dollars have shrunk in purchasing power. Recent
responses to emergency food requests have been
deferred until new harvests are in sight or have been
denied altogether. U.S. food aid decisions are now
made with one eye on the silo and the other on the
sky. Food aid, observed a Sri Lankan delegate at the
Conference, has become like a rich man's umbrella,
willingly shared with friends until it starts raining.

Political and military friends have benefited more
from U.S. food aid than others in greater need. In
1973, the United States refused credits for wheat
sales to the democratically elected socialist government of Chile under President Allende, only to press
them later on the military faction which overthrew
him. In 1974 almost half of our food aid went to
Southeast Asia, most of it to bolster regimes in South
Vietnam and Cambodia. In 1974, between seven and
eight times as much U.S. food aid went to Cambodia
as to Bangladesh. Congressional action now prohibits
the use for military purposes of currency generated
by selling food aid and sets a 30 percent limit on the
amount of U.S. food aid under Title I which can go
to countries not among those Most Seriously
Affected.

The World Food Conference agreed in principle on
a new philosophy of food aid. Rather than serving the
narrow political interests of donor countries, food aid
shall be provided and utilized for the emergency and
nutritional needs of poorer countries and for "stimulating rural employment through development

projects." It shall become a more thoroughly international resource provided by a wider range of donor
countries and with a larger percentage directed
through UN channels. (The UN World Food Program
has tended to be less political in operation than
bilateral food aid programs.) Donor governments have
pledged to contribute at least ten million tons of food
aid per year, a substantial increase over present levels.
Increased commitments have been announced by
Canada, Hungary, Japan, The Netherlands, New
Zealand, Norway, the United States and Yugoslavia.
They strengthen the larger system of world food
security and, in the absence of a network of well-
stocked national reserves, provide the ingredients of
an ongoing international resource to meet food
shortages.

The Conference was less successful in arranging
immediate food aid for people hungry during the first
six months of 1975. Despite new pledges for this
period, delegates returned home without having much
closed the gap of 7.5 million tons of food aid needed
for them. The missing 5 million tons, which could
imperil as many as 50 million people, was available
but neither contributed nor earmarked for those in
need. Various bilateral agreements (for example
between the U.S. and Bangladesh) which have since
been signed seem to have been too little and too late.

Action On Other Fronts

New action on population in the context of the
global food scene represents another promising development. At the World Population Conference in

Bucharest, governments placed changes in the rate of population growth within the context of economic and social development. The eventual leveling off of population growth was linked, in effect, to successful integrated rural development. Changes in attitudes toward marriage, family size and childbearing were seen to accompany increases in agricultural production, farm income and land ownership. For the immediate future, governments agreed to press "responsible parenthood" and to make family planning aid more available to those desiring it.

The World Food Conference honored these conclusions. It backed programs to achieve "a desirable balance between population and food supply" and emphasized the role of women as partners in food production and nutrition and in decisions about reproduction. It took seriously a warning from Pope Paul VI that "it is inadmissible that those who have control of the wealth and resources of mankind should try to resolve the problem of hunger by forbidding the poor to be born."

Will these measures reduce population growth? The chances are good but the uncertainties many. On the positive side, the long-range implications of current population trends are now better understood by governments. Some developing nations have already restrained high birth rates, including China, Sri Lanka, Cuba, South Korea and parts of India. (Others such as Brazil have embarked on programs with opposite goals.) Some rich countries are already increasing their aid to family planning programs in poorer lands. While the cost of making family planning services available to everyone wishing them is only about $2 billion annually, the real question is not the cost of the services but the broader socio-economic gains of which these are one important part. Creating fewer children, like producing more food, cannot be isolated from the fabric of society of which fertile parents and not-so-fertile lands are a part.

There is new hope for the hungry in the nutritional programs charted by the Conference. Developing countries have pledged national plans and priorities which will improve the nutritional health of their most needy people. Developed countries have offered their help in expanding health, education and feeding services, particularly through maternal and child health clinics and schools. U.S. Food for Peace commodities alone reached about 76 million persons in such programs in 1973. Countries contributing food and governmental and private agencies administering it have been asked to expand their efforts. The cost of a year's supplementary feeding is only $20 per child; $4 billion annually would feed the world's 200 million malnourished children. The UN is establishing a global nutrition surveillance system to monitor the situations of vulnerable groups in developing countries.

As for new economic relationships among nations, the hungry will find less hope in the Conference than in the UN Special Session on Raw Materials and Development held in April, 1974. There, nations came to grips with certain basic structural flaws in the world economy. "Rapid political, economic, social and technological developments," pointed out the Netherlands delegate, "have brought about unprecedented change in the relations among peoples. The world has entered into the age of interdependence. The interests of the few can no longer be isolated from the interests of the many; nor can the prosperity of the few be divorced from the poverty of the many." Despite this deepening interdependence, the international economic system has contributed, in UN Secretary General Waldheim's words, to a widening gap between "the worlds of affluence and poverty, frustration and opportunity, conspicuous consumption and destitution." Caught between declining terms of trade and shrinking aid, developing countries have in recent years become poorer and hungrier.

The Special Session's recommendations were of several kinds. A Declaration on the Establishment of a New International Economic Order affirms new relationships based on the economic interdependence of all countries, each of them sovereign and equal. The new order is to be ushered in with the help of a program of action to give developing countries more control over their raw materials, to help meet their basic food needs, and to restructure international trade along more equitable lines. To help them with food, fuel and other necessities, an emergency operation was set up. As of late 1974, it had made grants to eleven needy nations based on pledges or payments of almost $4 billion from 20 developed and oil-producing countries. The United States, with reserva-·· tions about the new order as well as the emergency operation, has yet to contribute. Canada has pledged $101 million. The Special Session underscored the importance of economic development and trade as permanent solutions of the crisis, though new ground rules for trade were not negotiated in detail.

The World Food Conference began where the Special Session left off, and finished at about the same point. Governments recognized that no farmer, whether living in a developed or a developing country, benefits from fluctuations in prices apart from an occasional windfall. All gain from access to each others' markets and from stable prices that bear a reasonable relationship to what they need to buy. No country is fully insulated from international economic forces which affect commodity prices, employment and living standards in all nations, though inflation can wreak more havoc in poor countries.

Therefore, the Conference asked international negotiations already underway to stabilize world markets, especially those for agricultural commodities, and to liberalize world trade, reducing restrictions which penalize poorer nations. International negotiations move slowly, however, and trade negotiations are particularly complex, affecting the heart of the world economic system which so many poorer countries experience as unjust. Thus today's hungry people are unlikely to benefit much from revamped economic relationships for at least five or six years.

The Future

These steps to deal with world hunger are constructive and promising. The world has taken the measure of the hunger crisis. It has begun to weave a multifaceted world food policy, based on a careful division of labor among participants. Integrated rural development in poorer countries is at the center, encompassing the basic improvements in the quality of life necessary for real headway on food and population matters. The poorest of the poor in developing nations have emerged as the focus of special concern. A system of world food security has been devised, along with measures for global nutrition surveillance, increased food aid and supplementary feeding. Some governments have made initial pledges to assist.

To say that these efforts are promising suggests that their success is by no means assured. International conferences do not produce food, nor do governments. People do. Conferences produce resolutions, and in this case some excellent ones. But governments must implement resolutions, deliver on pledges, honor commitments—in short, complete the weaving project. The need for comprehensive follow-up action tempers any optimism about an easy victory over hunger by 1985.

Ambassador Edwin Martin, Coordinator of the U.S. delegation, has said that six months should be long enough to determine whether the Conference has failed. By mid-1975, he believes, governments and the UN will either have run with the ball or dropped it. But a full five years will be needed to gauge the Conference's success. Why so long?

It was the first effort to map out a global food strategy. It will take some time to organize and get into

operation the follow-up institutions created. Designing
new plans giving a higher priority to food production,
and then preparing and carrying out investment projects
to implement them, have always been multiyear tasks.
Reaching small farmers scattered widely over the countryside with new technology they can use without un-
due risks, as well as getting them the financial and physical inputs usually required, has placed and will continue
to place a heavy strain on the personnel resources and
administrative capacities of most developing countries.
It will be especially important also to test what happens
if we have two or three years of good harvests. Will
complacency take over? Hence five years seems the very
earliest point at which it would be fair to conclude that
the Conference succeeded . . .

It is indeed a long way from the Conference in
Rome to Maize, Kansas; Estevan, Saskatchewan; Baramati, India; and Ouahigouya, Upper Volta. Farmers in
developed countries in the coming years will have to
make "an unusually complex set of production and
marketing decisions," says the U.S. Senate Agriculture Committee. In the United States, with acreage
restrictions removed, and in other developed countries, farmers "will be deciding for themselves what
and how much to plant. In making those decisions
they will have to carefully assess the availability of
fuel, fertilizer, credit, and other production inputs;
domestic and foreign demand; and relative profit-
ability of the various crops and livestock." Their
decisions are hardly a matter of simply consulting the
Farmer's Almanac.

Farmers in developing countries will be doing
their own calculations, perhaps in less complex
fashion, but along similar lines. If the World Food

Conference succeeds, these farmers will be better supplied with fuel and fertilizer, better advised in agricultural techniques, better equipped with improved tools, seeds, and credit, and better rewarded for their labors by domestic and world prices.

Out of such decisions there and here, influenced by personal attitudes and judgments, national policies and practices, and international factors, and affected by the weather and many other variables, will come future harvests. These are the real hope of the hungry.

4

the governments

At the World Food Conference, the governments of the world gave themselves new marching orders for the coming decade in a massive effort to provide new hope for the hungry. While few of these orders signal a complete about-face, many are promising and deserve a closer look.

All Governments

Governments have accepted the world food crisis as a global problem soluble only if nations act together. What U.S. Secretary of State Kissinger called "the accelerating momentum of our inter-dependence" has led to strategies based on coopera-tion rather than confrontation. All governments are now obliged to chart their new course more fully through international institutions. With such support, the new World Food Council can do its job of overseeing the completion of the giant weaving project.

The misgivings of some nations about international institutions in general and the UN in particular are thus cause for concern. The United States and several

other developed countries find bilateral dealings with
poorer countries more efficient and politically useful.
UN channels tend to be slower, more complex and
more anonymous than two-way arrangements
between, for example, the Federal Republic of Germany and Brazil. Some developing countries themselves find UN agencies bureaucratic, unresponsive
and, in their own way, political. The U.S. government
has deeper misgivings as well, alleging domination of
the UN by "a tyranny of the majority" of developing
countries over the minority of developed ones.
"Many Americans are questioning their belief in the
UN," Ambassador Scali told the General Assembly in
December, 1974. "They are deeply disturbed." The
cartoon in Chapter 5 comments on his statement.

Nonetheless, all nations have a stake in the continued and improved functioning of the UN system.
How can world hunger be eradicated without world
food security? How can world food security become
real without world food reserves? How can world
food reserves be built if nations weave their own rugs
individually, or in pairs, or in blocs, rather than
working together? The world food crisis is "a global
problem involving the whole human community," the
New Zealand delegate told the World Food Conference. "It cannot be treated as if it were compart-
mented into a series of national problems." Nor,
added the Argentinian delegate, can it be placed "in a
watertight compartment as if it had nothing to do
with the major political, financial, social and cultural
problems of the day."

The need for global approaches means not the end

of bilateral aid, but the fuller utilization and strengthening, where necessary, of UN channels. The purpose of aid, after all, is not to win friends but to solve problems, and some problems can clearly be solved better jointly than otherwise. The satisfaction of having helped stem hunger or poverty or pollution is its own reward. The glory of the Marshall Plan after World War II was not that it was American but that it helped Europe back onto its feet. The United States and other countries must not get out of the UN but rather participate more fully through it in a common attack on world hunger.

All governments share a second post-Rome responsibility: the massive shifting of resources toward integrated rural development. For developing countries, this will mean redirecting funds from industrial and other uses to agricultural needs; for developed countries, substantially increased development assistance.

Is this financially possible without a broad cut in military expenditures? Governments in 1973 spent about $275 billion for arms. More than one tenth of this was spent by developing countries themselves. Developed countries pay about twenty dollars for arms for every dollar of development aid. Unheeded remains a recent UN General Assembly resolution calling on the big powers to reduce their military expenditures by 10 percent to free money for investment in development. A World Food Conference resolution along similar lines may await the same fate.

Which route to national security represents the best investment of scarce funds? Proliferating world hunger threatens world peace and stability. "Mega-

deaths from famine are no less terrible than the
slaughter of war," the Rome Forum's distinguished
participants told the World Food Conference. "They
require the same political effort and authority to hold
them at bay." West German Chancellor Willy Brandt
told the UN General Assembly that "morally it makes
no difference whether a man is killed in war or is
condemned to starve to death by the indifference of
others." A world food policy which eradicates hunger
may provide more genuine security than nuclear
stockpiles and conventional weapons arsenals.

Viewed against current military expenditures,
world food policy costs appear very modest indeed.
Chart 4 shows that the recommended 10 percent
reduction in world military expenditures would more
than meet the cost of everything proposed by the
World Food Conference. Several years ago, when
world military expenditures were "only" $200 billion
annually, that figure was more than the combined
income of 1.8 billion of the world's poor people. The
world is nickling and diming its way to integrated
rural development while the big money goes elsewhere, ignoring the wisdom of the old Anabaptist
saying, "The fairest weapon man can wield is the
plow in the farmer's field."

Will sufficient funds be available for plowshares
and pruning hooks until allocations for swords and
spears have been trimmed? This book does not
undertake to resolve that question. Suffice it to point
out that all governments have a stake in massively
increased funds for agricultural development. The
most available source of funds at the scale needed is

doubtless current world military expenditures. Trimming back spears would seem an investment in global peace and justice which military weapons themselves cannot buy. In the words of the Zambian delegate, "let us range the army of humanity behind its general—the farmer."

Governments in Developing Countries

Conditions vary widely. Thailand, Argentina, Mexico and Burma are net exporters of food; other developing countries are net food importers. The Sudan, Indonesia and the Philippines have vast areas of sparsely settled land; Bangladesh and Haiti have more people than space. South Korea and China have trimmed population growth rates; Brazil is encouraging human fertility. Some developing countries have capitalist, others socialist economies; some are democracies, others dictatorships. Some poor nations are rich in natural resources; others are poor in that sense as well. Some have good communication and transportation; others are isolated and landlocked. Nonetheless, most of them, thanks to the World Food Conference, share certain common marching orders.

The first, following from what has already been said, is to refocus their priorities toward integrated rural development. For the many nations which have patterned past efforts according to the capital, technology and expertise available in trade and aid from richer countries, this means some major readjustments. Dr. Philip Potter, general secretary of the World Council of Churches, posed the challenge to the Conference.

CHART 4: PLOWSHARES AND SWORDS*

Estimated annual costs of implementing World Food Conference recommendations (above current expenditures).

Roughly comparable military expenditures.

OVERALL COSTS

$12 billion annually for each of the next ten years (for increased food production, fertilizer, water and land resources development, research and technology, rural credit, and other essentials to step up developing country food production)

$12 billion is less than 5% of the world military expenditures of $269 billion in 1973. $12 billion is about 13% of the proposed US Defense Budget of $94 billion for 1976 and of the estimated 1974 USSR Defense Budget of $96 billion.

$8 billion annually is roughly the share of developing countries toward this goal.

$8 billion is less than 20% of the $42 billion spent by developing countries for military expenditures in 1973.

$4 billion annually is roughly the share of developed countries toward this goal.

$4 billion is less than 2% of the $227 billion spent by developed countries for military expenditures in 1973.

$16-18 billion: the annual purchase price for the grain likely to be needed by developing countries should they fail to increase their own food production at the target rate of 3.5-4.0% per year.

$16 billion is about 6% of the world military expenditures in 1973. It is about 19% of the $85.2 billion US Defense Budget for 1973. Estimates of the USSR Defense Budget for 1973 range from $34-$86 billion.

SELECTED COMPONENT PARTS

$8.0 billion: Annual cost of the necessary water and land development in all developing countries.

$8.0 billion is the cost to the USSR of almost 600,000 servicemen for a year. (Russia's total manpower of 2.3 million servicemen in 1973 cost an estimated $30.8 billion.) $8 billion is less than 40% of the cost of the 244 B-1 bombers planned by the US Department of Defense to replace its B-52 bomber fleet.

$4.0 billion is 10 percent of the 1973 military expenditures of the 13 NATO countries (excluding the US). It is about 60 percent of the 1973 military expenditures of the six Warsaw Pact countries (excluding the USSR).

$1.2 billion is the cost of the U.S. Navy's LHA ship-building program which is producing five helicopter-carrying assault ships "to carry combat forces to attack third world countries or to Europe in support of a NATO war," if necessary.

$.5 billion is the cost of 48 Phantom and Skyhawk fighter bombers purchased by Israel from the U.S. for 1976 delivery.

$.7 billion is the cost of about 500 helicopters purchased by Iran from the U.S. for 1975-76 delivery.

$6.0 billion is the cost of the U.S. Poseidon missile system now under production, a system of 31 subs and 4960 nuclear weapons whose purpose is "nuclear attack on USSR and China," if necessary.

$2 billion is somewhat less than the 1973 military budget of Canada of $2.4 billion and of India of $2.3 billion and slightly more than the Rumanian military budget of $1.8 billion.

$4.5 billion is the cost of the U.S. C5A aircraft program which is building 81 military jet cargo transport planes "to transport equipment and supplies to foreign bases".

$1.6 billion is the cost of 600 aircraft in the Air Force's AX program, now in the R & D stage, nuclear weapons designed to "attack enemies in third world countries," if necessary.

$4.0 billion: Annual cost of supplementary feeding for the world's 200 million malnourished children. (An undisputed need but not a Conference commitment.)

$1.2 billion: Annual cost of the necessary farmers' credit program for marketing, storage, and revolving funds in all developing countries.

$1.2 billion: Annual cost of the necessary agricultural research.

$.5 billion: Annual purchases of the necessary fertilizer for developing countries.

RELATED SOCIAL NEEDS (Not World Food Conference Recommendations)

$4.0 billion: Doubling of world medical research

$2.0 billion: Provision of family planning services universally

$4-5 billion: Elimination of hunger in the United States

$1.5 billion: Elimination of world wide illiteracy over 5-year period

*This chart has been compiled by the author based on information from the sources listed in "For Further Reference."

As a person coming from the Caribbean, I want to say a few words to the representatives of the governments of the Third World. While recognizing the fact that we are victims of international injustice, maintained and promoted by the present economic order, I must confess that our own governments as well as rich and powerful groups in our countries, share a heavy responsibility in contributing to the present crisis. Within our countries we have done little to reduce the gap between the rich and the poor. We have neglected the poorest sectors of our society. We have been aping the development models of the rich nations, which are irrelevant to our social, economic and cultural realities. We have worked in collusion with foreign interests to exploit the poor masses, and in so doing have adopted colonial or neo-colonial patterns of behaviour. Without adopting radical measures to change the structures in our society and adopting authentic goals and processes of development, we do not earn the right to criticize the rich and powerful elsewhere or the moral credibility and courage to propose and effect changes in the global order.

The reordering of priorities in favor of agriculture has implications for land reform, land use, and technology. How governments of poor countries follow up on their pledge and distribute land more equitably is a function of their own situations. The challenge is not only to make more land available to the poor. Unless more democratic patterns of land tenure are followed up with support for the new beneficiaries, food production and income can shrink rather than swell.

Developing country governments have accepted the need for a new approach to land use and technology, one suited to small farms and ordinary people in search of work. In many poor countries, "small is beautiful." In the Philippines, rice production was one third greater on sample farms of 5 acres or less than on farms twice or more as large. Developing countries usually lack the economies of scale which have led to larger units of production, marketing, and distribution in industrialized nations. Many do best when they use "appropriate technology," meaning not always harvesters, combines, and chemical fertilizers but improved tools, plows, and organic fertilizer. (The cartoon in Chapter 6 speaks to the point.) Given the difficulty of reaching one million villages and one hundred million small farmers with these improvements, it is no wonder that large-scale agriculture has worked its seductive spell on many unsuspecting nations.

Many countries are being approached by agribusiness companies with large-scale agricultural schemes. Past performance suggests that these projects, for all of their appeal, may not in the long run make the best use of land or people. Many are designed to produce luxury and export foods like tomato paste and citrus fruit rather than essential and locally needed foods such as cereal grains. The UN thus warns that "projects which make new lands available to large foreign or local companies for a rapid increase in production with the help of most modern machines and techniques may produce more food, but may not solve the problems of poverty and unemployment of the people in the region unless accompanied by special measures for them."

At the heart of the shift of priorities toward agriculture, then, is a concern for "people mobilization."

World hunger is not a purely technical problem to be handled by tinkering with technical inputs. "Agriculture gets energy from the sun," writes someone from Pakistan, "but agricultural development gets its drive from persons." "The world food crisis will not be solved," Pope Paul VI reminded the Conference, "without the participation of the agricultural workers."

The Conference agreed. "Human resources are the most important resources the developing countries have." (In fact, it is somewhat misleading to speak of developing countries as "poor." They are rich in people and, some of them, in the natural resources on which resource-poor developed countries increasingly depend.) The Conference decided that "the involvement of the people, particularly the underprivileged and the poorest among them, in the process of economic and social development" is indispensable to producing more food. "Unless and until that [involvement] is achieved, the technology, fertilizer, or available water and other resources will not be utilized adequately or efficiently; the food that is produced will not be distributed equitably; and the entire structure of the rural society will remain under the stresses of growing unemployment and undiminished hunger."

Methods of human resource mobilization differ. Communes, farmer's movements, kibbutzim, ujamaa villages, cooperatives, community action agencies and many other grass roots structures have been developed in one place or another. People thus organized at the local level turn to governments not for bureaucrats but for agricultural extension agents, community organizers, animators, medical parapro- fessionals, applied nutritionists, cottage industry administrators, borers of wells. One person with practical skills who is prepared to work and live in a remote village is generally worth a dozen visiting uni- versity professors and business tycoons.

Despite governmental pledges at the Conference in Rome to mobilize people at the village level, it would be naive to assume that this will happen auto- matically. Such changes of government priorities and policies are by definition political changes, the more so when they involve reforms in the very ways governments operate and societies are structured. The Office of Economic Opportunity (OEO) stirred up such controversy in trying to change the structures hamstringing the poor in the U.S. that the War on Poverty ended pretty much in a cease-fire. Even the OEO requirement that the poor be involved in mak- ing decisions about priorities and programs affecting them encountered heavy resistance. Human resource mobilization has few universally applicable blue- prints; only the objective that people be involved in improving their own lives is common to diverse situations on every continent. Such are the critical choices about the use of people, land, and external aid which confront developing countries and cry out for resolution by them.

Among the developing countries, the thirteen members of the Organization of Petroleum Exporting Countries (OPEC) form something of a special group. Their new wealth gives them new opportunity to meet their own developmental agendas at home and to purchase what they need abroad. In the view of many, their wealth now confers "special responsibilities" on them to assist other countries, particularly those hardest hit by higher fuel bills.

OPEC countries have already begun to reach out in the suggested fashion. Iran, Iraq and the United Arab Emirates are supplying India with fuel on deferred payment terms. Bangladesh has received aid from three OPEC nations. Three of them aided Pakistan after its recent earthquake. Iraq is helping build a fertilizer plant in India, Abu Dhabi in Pakistan. Kuwait is financing agricultural development in Brazil, and pledged fertilizer to the neediest nations at Rome. Nigeria has pledged funds for agricultural research and Saudi Arabia has granted them to the UN's World Food Program. Libya and Algeria have contributed to the African Development Bank. OPEC countries have proposed a new International Fund for Agricultural Development, to which they and others will now apparently contribute. Six OPEC countries have aided the UN Emergency Operation for the Most Seriously Affected nations, including a $1.5 billion pledge from Iran. The list could go on.

Some critics, perhaps unaware of these actions, pledged or delivered, have suggested that until the OPEC nations have stepped up their efforts, others should freeze their development contributions at current levels. While increased voluntary OPEC aid may be forthcoming, the Gross National Products (GNP) of many oil producing nations on a per person basis, despite their new wealth, remain far less than those of developed countries. Several have already pledged a larger proportion of development aid per citizen than have developed nations. Kuwait's 1974 pledged aid was at more than 5 percent of its Gross National Product, as compared with aid delivered of about two tenths of 1 percent for the United States. OPEC wealth cannot singlehandedly solve the world food crisis any more than can U.S. or Canadian grain. Even purchasing North American grain with OPEC petrodollars would be no panacea. There is no substitute for increased aid by developed nations.

Developed Country Governments

"If the governments of the developing world—who must measure the risks of reform against the risks of revolution—are prepared to exercise the requisite political will to assault the problem of poverty in the countryside," writes Mr. Robert McNamara of the World Bank, "then the governments of the wealthy nations must display equal courage." Their marching orders are to support the efforts of developing countries to do the things we have just described. Such support has several dimensions.

Official development assistance, or "foreign aid," needs enlarging and refocusing. Official development assistance refers basically to developmental rather than military aid provided by governments. In recent years, as Chart 4 indicates, such aid has not even held its own against inflation. Only Sweden contributes .7 percent of its Gross National Product for aid, the goal established by governments for the UN's Second Development Decade (1970-1980). The United

States, which conceives of itself as a generous nation, in 1975 slips to fifteenth of seventeen western nations in proportionate contributions to development. Dr. Barbara Ward's comments at the Synod of Catholic Bishops in Rome in 1971 are scarcely less true today. "A number of the wealthiest nations appear steadily less committed, less concerned and less inventive in their approach to world development." In the absence of more commitment and imagination, those in absolute porverty in the Most Seriously Affected nations will not benefit from aid at all.

Perhaps a good place to start in the United States would be to find a term more in keeping with global interdependence than "foreign aid." Aid also needs refocusing on rural development, a target now specified in the U.S. Foreign Assistance Act of 1973. Canada and other governments are also reviewing aid to increase the share spent on agricultural dev lopment. The World Bank and its International Development Agency are devoting more attention to s farmers during the period 1975-80.

Aid in these revised forms can do a better job of helping to mobilize human resources. It can fund credit access projects, education and training ventures, rural cooperatives and other essentials in the process of transition to new patterns of land ownership and utilization. The initiative for requesting and using such outside help, however, belongs to developing countries themselves. Developed nations should sometimes even stay out of the way altogether, given a track record in which their "aid" has solidified inequities rather than brought liberation to the captives.

Secondly, in a world of scarce inputs as well as scarce cash, developed countries should adjust their consumption and allocation patterns to assure that food and fertilizer are available to countries in maximum need. Grain for shipment to the neediest nations could become more available if two related actions were taken. First, reduced consumption of meat products in wealthier countries would liberate grain for other uses and would cushion whatever inflationary impact on domestic prices large scale government grain purchases for overseas use might have. Secondly, some arrangements by governments to earmark grain for the neediest countries would prevent its loss to commercial buyers. A system in which grain goes to the highest bidder reinforces the malnutrition of those without money to buy.

The fertilizer situation is so tight that domestic and overseas commercial demand seems likely to exceed supply for several years. Reduced fertilizer use in developed countries is thus clearly in order. The cartoon which follows comments on the subject. Fertilizer for non-food producing uses such as lawns and golf courses runs to about three million tons in the United States each year. Developing countries in 1974 failed to meet their needs due to short supply and high prices by about two million tons. India's shortfall alone was estimated at one million tons. Perhaps even the use of fertilizer for food production itself in developed countries should be balanced against what the same nutrients could do when applied in develop-

MARGULIES

Margulies, a ROTHCO Original

ing countries. U.S. Agriculture Secretary Butz has said that with demand for food up on all sides, "the world food market will be our oyster." While developed country food production can help meet the emergency needs of poorer countries for food (although that is frequently not the use to which such food is put), rich country oysters should not grow pearls at the expense of food production in poorer nations.

Some basic adjustments of both governmental and individual practice in developed countries are thus needed. Ways must be found so that scarce resources such as food and fertilizer are not only saved from consumption in wealthier nations and from commercial export elsewhere, but also transferred to points of greatest human need.

The United States, for example, currently has no national policy or administrator to draw together all of

CHART 5. Flow of Official Development Assistance
Measured as a Percentage of Gross National Product

INDIVIDUAL COUNTRIES (Selected)	1960	1965	1970	1971	1972	1973	1974	1975	1980
Canada	.19	.19	.42	.42	.47	.43	.51	.51	
Germany	.31	.40	.32	.34	.31	.32	.30	.28	
Japan	.24	.27	.23	.23	.21	.25	.24	.24	
Norway	.11	.16	.32	.33	.41	.45	.63	.65	
Sweden	.05	.19	.38	.44	.48	.56	.69	.70	
Switzerland	.04	.09	.15	.11	.21	.15	.15	.15	
United Kingdom	.56	.47	.37	.41	.39	.35	.34	.32	
United States	.53	.49	.31	.32	.29	.23	.21	.20	
GRAND TOTAL									
ODA $ in millions (current prices)	4665	5895	6832	7762	8671	9415	10706	11948	24400
ODA 1973 prices	7660	9069	9346	9976	10059	9415	9391	9452	13480
ODA as % of GNP	.52	.44	.34	.35	.34	.30	.30	.29	.30

This chart is adapted from one accompanying the 1974 address of Mr. Robert McNamara to the Board of Governors of the World Bank, which was based in turn on data supplied by the Organization for Economic Cooperation and Development (OECD). Since the developed socialist and oil-producing countries are not members of the OECD, comparable data for them is not included. In 1973, the U.S. ranked 14th of the 17 OECD countries in its relative contributions to development. (Only 8 of those 17 countries are shown here.) The projected U.S. 1975 development assistance rate of .20% of GNP compares with the 2.79% rate in 1949 at the beginning of the Marshall Plan. The 1980 figures are estimates by the World Bank of what would be required to achieve a GNP growth rate of 2.1% per year in the Most Seriously Affected nations.

the pieces of the food puzzle, including domestic and commercial demand, the needs of American farmers and their overseas counterparts, and the needs of the hungry at home and abroad. American farmers who have a right to a reasonable return on their investments would surely be willing to harmonize their efforts as part of a national world food production policy. Yet when the farmers dramatize their agony by killing livestock or withdrawing acreage from production, the public, saddled already with high food prices, views them as culprits and misanthropes rather than as victims of a food policy vacuum. There is no substitute for a U.S. food policy, fully integrated into global realities, as a means of dealing with fluctuating prices and demand. Who shall plant and who shall reap, like who shall live and who shall die, must be a matter of policy and not solely of the price mechanism, particularly if food production in developed countries is to combat malnutrition elsewhere.

Thirdly, developed country governments need to adapt their economic lives more fully to the realities of economic interdependence. Equitable prices for raw materials may mean higher prices for consumer goods. Developing country products, granted access to developed nation markets, may require adjustments in employment patterns there. If food can be produced in poorer nations more cheaply and securely than elsewhere, this should be encouraged even at the possible expense of food exporting developed countries. Without carefully conceived governmental action, however, the effects of such adjustments on individual farmers, workers and consumers in developed nations could be severely unsettling.

Developed countries bring different resources to a global food policy and must make different adjustments to it. The United States, which has no governmentally controlled grain reserves, and Norway, which does, will proceed differently. Food importers like Russia and Japan and food exporters like Canada and Australia face different challenges. Yugoslavia and Rumania, which in the past have done little with food aid, and Holland and Sweden which have contributed substantially, will respond differently. Yet the adjustments to be made in Washington and Oslo, Moscow and Tokyo, Ottawa and Canberra, Belgrade and Bucharest, Amsterdam and Stockholm are, all things considered, not an onus but a boon.

All nations, developed and developing alike, stand to gain from these various yet integrated marching orders. All will benefit from a world undergirded by a global approach to the eradication of hunger and malnutrition, and, looking ahead further still, from a world without hunger or malnutrition at all. All need to exercise a new level of political will and restraint, individually and collectively, if that goal is to be attained.

5

churches and
private organizations

We have concentrated our attention thus far on responses to the world food crisis by governments and UN agencies. These are only part of the picture, admittedly the major part. The World Food Conference has also called upon "all peoples expressing their will as individuals, and through their governments and non-governmental organizations, to work together to bring about the end of the age-old scourge of hunger."

It is to these organizations that we now turn. Following an overview of the private agencies involved in the meeting of world hunger, we shall turn in more detail to the efforts of the churches in the areas of program operation, development education, and the influencing of public policy. Examples of these activities are the subject of Chapter 6.

An Overview

The magnitude of private voluntary contributions to overseas development is remarkable. In 1973, when official development assistance from developed countries totaled about $9.4 billion, private funds from those countries added an extra $1.4 billion. U.S.

private contributions in that year were at the aston-
ishingly high level of about thirty cents for each
dollar of U.S. government development aid ($905
million compared with almost $3 billion). U.S. per
capita giving is among the highest for developed
countries, whereas in government aid the United
States, as we know from the previous chapter, ranks
among the lowest. Domestic priorities and problems
notwithstanding, the American people still contribute
substantial private resources for humanitarian assistance.

Channels for private contributions are diverse.
Most funds go to and through nonprofit agencies such
as those listed in Chart 6. A listing published in late
1974 by the American Council of Voluntary Agencies
shows some 152 such organizations involved in food
production and agricultural assistance abroad. Countless others are engaged in other activities as well in
fields such as health, education, economic development and refugee resettlements. Each agency, according to its own broad goals, develops or supports programs in various countries. Some agencies depend
largely on direct individual contributions; others are
supported by organizations, groups, denominations or
foundations.

In addition to private funds, many agencies administer government monies. For a number of years, the
Canadian, Scandinavian and West German governments have given funds to voluntary agencies for use
in overseas programs. Most U.S. government support
has been limited to the Food for Peace program and
to contracts and grants for specific projects. Re-

cently, however, the Agency for International Development has broadened the basis for grants to private U.S. agencies and increased the sums available.

Private organizations have varying policies and practices regarding food and funds available from governments. Development agencies in Canada and Sweden receive substantial governmental sums with few strings attached. In three Canadian provinces, private donated funds are matched by provincial governments, and then the total is matched by the federal government, with private agency programs the direct beneficiary. In the U.S., CARE, one of the largest overseas relief agencies, received about 83 percent of its total 1973 program value of $123 million from the U.S. government, the balance from private contributors. The American Friends Service Committee, on the other hand, uses no government funds in its overseas programs.

In addition to private voluntary agencies, foundations are major facilitators of overseas development. Of the $905 million in contributions from the U.S. private sector in 1973, something over $150 million came from foundations. While foundations have various priorities, a number have made sizeable investments in the area of agricultural research and its application. The Ford Foundation concentrates its overseas activities on increasing food production, strengthening educational systems, improving the planning and execution of development programs, and reducing excessive population growth. The Rockefeller Foundation stresses the conquest of hunger, the problems of population, and university development. Together, these two foundations were instrumental in underwriting the research which produced the new strains of wheat and rice of the Green Revolution in the 1960s. They currently contribute to an international network of research centers in developing regions where work is proceeding on improved varieties of various crops and their dissemination to farmers. The Ford-Rockefeller contributions in 1973 to overseas efforts in these fields totalled $64 million.

Church Efforts in Program Operation

There are many agencies which express the concerns of Christians in the United States for people in developing countries. Among the major ones, Church World Service operates relief and development programs overseas on behalf of the 31 member Protestant and Orthodox denominations and 40 million persons associated with the National Council of Churches. Lutheran World Relief serves a similar function for the three national Lutheran churches and their nine million members. The counterpart agency for the National Association of Evangelicals, with a constituency of about 40 million persons, is the World Relief Commission. Catholic Relief Services is the comparable agency for the 48 million member Roman Catholic community.

In addition, many Protestant, Orthodox, Evangelical, and Catholic denominations have their own individual outreach agencies such as the United Church Board for World Ministries, The Seventh Day Adventist World Service, and the Maryknoll Fathers.

There are also non-denominational Christian agencies, one of the largest of which is World Vision International. The situation is roughly the same in Canada.

The American Jewish community reaches out to Jews around the world in need of relief, reconstruction and rehabilitation primarily through the American Jewish Joint Distribution Committee. Most of its funds come from the United Jewish Appeal, which raises more than 20 percent of all U.S. private funds donated for overseas use.

For more than a century the churches have sought, with varying degrees of effectiveness and sensitivity, to meet the needs of poor and oppressed people throughout the world without reference to their religious persuasion. In a sense, governments at the World Food Conference "got religion" by turning their attention to those with whom the churches have been working all along. We shall focus on the hunger efforts of Church World Service (CWS) and Lutheran World Relief (LWR), whose work is somewhat typical of other agencies as well.

CWS and LWR were founded in the mid-1940s to deal with the refugee needs of post-war Europe. More recently, their attention turned to developing countries and, more recently still, to the Most Seriously Affected nations (MSAs). Both agencies have responded to natural and man-made disasters, providing emergency food, medicines, blankets, shelter, and personnel in such areas as Bangladesh, India, the Sudan, Niger, Nigeria, Vietnam, Nicaragua, Honduras and Peru.

They have also become increasingly active in

integrated rural development, particularly in education, health and family planning, agriculture and
water resources. In 1973, 15 percent of CWS funds
went toward immediate relief needs, 30 percent
toward reconstruction during the period of 3 to 24
months after disasters, and 55 percent toward
development projects unrelated to disasters. LWR is
refocusing its efforts in response to the global hunger
situation. Its revised strategy supports "projects
aimed at breaking basic constraints that prevent
developing countries from helping the poorest majority. It envisages efforts that develop skills and
competencies needed by the poor to become self-sufficient."

CWS and LWR, rather than initiating and operating programs of their own, usually respond to
requests from counterpart agencies such as the
Christian Commission for Development in Bangladesh
and Diaconia in Brazil. They also cooperate closely
with counterpart agencies in developed countries,
such as Canadian Lutheran World Relief and Brot für
die Welt of Germany. At the regional level they stay
closely in touch with regional church bodies, such as
the Christian Conference of Asia and the All Africa
Conference of Churches. At the international level
they are associated with the World Council of
Churches and the Lutheran World Federation. Frequently their efforts are linked to those of Catholic
Relief Services and Caritas Internationalis. They are
a world-wide Christian response to human need.

In 1973, CWS supported programs valued at $23.5
million in about 40 countries, 15 of them on the

CHART 6

Sample National and International Voluntary Agencies Involved in Program Operation

Africare
American Friends Service Committee
American Jewish Joint Distribution Committee
Brethren Service Committee
Canadian Catholic Organization for Development & Peace
(Canadian) Interchurch Fund for International Development
Canadian Lutheran World Relief
Canadian University Service Overseas
CARE (Cooperative for American Relief Everywhere)

Catholic Relief Services
Church World Service
CODEL (Coordination in Development)
Community Development Foundation
Community Nutrition Institute
Heifer Project International
Lutheran World Federation
Lutheran World Relief
Mennonite Central Committee
Organization for Rehabilitation Training
Oxfam
Save the Children Federation

Seventh-day Adventist World Service
Technoserve
The (Mississippi) Delta Ministry
The Salvation Army
The World Council of Churches
The World Relief Commission
The Young Men's and Young Women's Christian Associations
Volunteers in Technical Assistance
World Vision International

Addresses of agencies based in the U.S. are available from the American Council of Voluntary Agencies, 200 Park Avenue South, New York, N.Y. 10015. Information on Canadian agencies is available from the Canadian Council for International Cooperation, 75 Sparks Street, Ottawa, Ontario, Canada, K1P 5B5. Information on voluntary agencies operating programs in various developing countries may be obtained from the International Council on Voluntary Agencies, 17 Avenue de la Paix, 1202 Geneva, Switzerland.

MSA list. LWR efforts, at $7.5 million, centered in more than 20 countries, including 5 MSAs. Whether in MSAs or elsewhere, both agencies try to seek out the forgotten people in the out-of-the-way places who are not touched by the efforts of governments or other voluntary agencies. Projects in the East African nation of Mauritius, for example, assist fishermen and their families on remote islands in the Indian Ocean.

CWS and LWR administer modest amounts of food aid under the U.S. Food for Peace program, but it is Catholic Relief Services and CARE, with more than 90 percent of the voluntary agency share between them, who are the chief administrators. CWS and LWR reduced their dependence on Food for Peace commodities even before the commodity supply shrank in the early 1970s, seeking instead a more broadly based approach to development. Like CRS and CARE, however, they use food commodities wherever possible in food-for-work and other developmental fashions. As of early 1975, they are negotiating grants for overseas programs with the U.S. Agency for International Development.

The strengths and weaknesses of CWS and LWR are in some ways typical of other private efforts and therefore merit a bit of attention. Their approach is a person-to-person one, concentrating on flexible and creative responses to grass roots human needs as determined by people themselves, frequently at the village level. The goal is not simply to provide social services, important though they be, but to incorporate these into broader efforts to deal with the root causes of hunger, mobilizing local resources wherever possible. Cornmeal, clothing and blankets, though indispensable in certain situations, are less important than seeds, plows and sewing machines. Self-help, leadership development and empowerment are at the heart of the effort, with all outside personnel and material resources tailored to those ends.

CWS and LWR programs have tended to be modest, small-scale and low-profile, spending modest amounts of money with maximum impact. In recent years, however, international ecumenical responses have made possible some programs in the million dollar range. A three-year program valued at $7.5 million is now underway in Bangladesh, with priority being given to agricultural development. Whatever a program's scale, administrative expenses are kept to a minimum. And, large or small, some successful programs have served as models for replication by governments; some failures have succeeded in pointing governments in other directions.

While CWS and LWR work closely with host governments, their involvement with people at the grass roots level lessens some of the political and bureaucratic entanglements that efforts by outside governments sometimes encounter. They have perhaps greater freedom than do governments to terminate their efforts if conditions develop which make their objectives unattainable. By working with local colleagues, CWS and LWR tap into the networks of relationships already existing in developing countries. They seek to strengthen local groups, religious and otherwise, reinforcing economic and social change from the inside in ways not generally open to governments. Their broad independence from the U.S. government frees them to respond to human need where it exists, as for example among the Liberation Movements in Africa.

Their weaknesses are, in a sense, the flipside of their strengths. Their efforts, while generally rooted in the decision-making processes of local communities, appear somewhat uneven because the needs to which they respond vary from place to place. Unlike governments, they do not try to be uniform in what they provide. Rather than furnishing supplies for every village school or medications for every dispensary in a given area, they may concentrate supplies and training or personnel in some places and provide very little elsewhere.

Seeking to facilitate rather than to administer, CWS and LWR efforts are very much caught up in the strengths and weaknesses of local leadership. Where local leadership is weak, program scale may remain modest. Even where local leadership is strong, overkill can be a danger. Church funds, despite the best of intentions, can, like government funds, subvert rather than support. They can easily reflect the agendas of outsiders rather the priorities of the people themselves. One national Christian council in Asia has been criticized by members who share its concerns about hunger for pursuing development projects to the neglect of the theological and practical needs of local congregations. And, while it is easy for agencies like CWS and LWR to increase dramatically their emergency relief activities as need arises, the expansion of developmental assistance programs in ways which

include local people in the process is a slower and
more complex undertaking. Funds for development
received in New York today cannot usually be
deployed in the service of development in a remote
Latin American village tomorrow.

While CWS and LWR projects are generally creative and constructive, their impact is limited by the
scale of their resources and is often not felt beyond a
certain geographical area. Although the necessary
contacts are developed with governments, programs
often do not influence the planning and priority-set-
ting process of developing countries at the highest
levels. Even so, their development assistance is welcomed by host governments and is now focussing
more sharply than ever on the persistent problem of
hunger and related ills. While the magnitude of their
involvement may seem small compared to governmental and intergovernmental efforts, CWS and LWR
programs by and large have won the respect of
knowledgeable international observers for their re-
sponsiveness and impact over a period of years.

No one contends that the churches individually
and jointly are doing enough. In fact, they themselves
have concluded, as have governments about their own
efforts, that "the sum total of existing church
programs matches neither the magnitude of the
problem nor the churches' potential resources." The
National Council of Churches and some of its
member denominations have therefore pledged "to
make hunger a priority issue in every local church and

community (and) to meet the immediate needs, locally and worldwide, in a more intensive and intentional way."

Contributions for programs were up in 1974, with many instances of new levels of giving by individuals, families, congregations and denominations. Many denominations which raise their basic support for CWS programs and other overseas activities through an annual Lenten appeal such as the One Great Hour of Sharing have noted an increase in giving. The Reformed Church in America's funds for hunger and development in 1974 were up almost three-fold over the previous year. Contributions in 1974 to the United Methodist Church, another member denomination of CWS, were up by 50 percent over 1973. CROP, the Community Hunger Appeal of CWS, reported substantial increase in funds for 1974.

Appeals within the three major American Lutheran churches in late 1974 have generated contributions for world hunger of over $4 million above and beyond normal giving. The Pennsylvania and Maryland Synods of the Lutheran Church in America have set goals of $500,000 each for world hunger fund raising. Special appeals for hunger have been well received by the general public as well. Contributions to CARE in 1974 were up 42 percent over the previous year.

While private agencies are expanding their programs, they point out that even vastly stepped-up private efforts can never substitute for expanded governmental development assistance. The orders of magnitude are different. CWS and LWR used contributions in late 1974 to purchase 3,000 tons of wheat for projects in India at a cost of about $550,000. Yet India's needs were in the millions of tons.

Stepped-up support by Christians of development efforts is the thrust of a new institution created by the World Council of Churches. Urging that 2 percent of the income of church organizations go to development and justice concerns, particularly world hunger, it has formed an Ecumenical Development Cooperative Society, a sort of churches' world bank. This will use investment capital from congregations and denominations in various countries to provide technical assistance and credit loans to the poorest people in developing nations. Churches can thus invest funds in socially responsible ways to provide start-up capital for self-help schemes of economic growth and social justice. The World Council has also called on churches and mission boards to give over their ample lands in developing countries to cooperative food production. The Lutheran World Federation noted in early 1975 an increase in requests from local churches in poorer nations for development assistance and has urged its members to respond.

The Churches and Development Education

The world food crisis needs not only new programs for the hungry, but new understandings among the well-fed. Our economic and political interdependence has accelerated faster than our grasp of it. Unless a new vision of these realities takes root and is followed up with changes in life styles suited to global interdependence, the underlying imbalances may remain unaffected. Again, a variety of religious (not to mention secular) agencies are dealing with the issue.

The churches have wrestled on many occasions with the question of how best to educate members of the imperatives of development and global justice.

In December, 1974, Protestants addressed the issue in a work session at the Graymoor Christian Unity Center. Viewing the educational task of the churches, they asked, "How can Americans be mobilized without on the one hand resorting to appeals for simplistic solutions which leave the basic problems untouched, or on the other, paralyzing them from action by overwhelming them with the problem's magnitude and complexity?" The work session resulted in a Graymoor Covenant which pledged "to mount a massive educational effort that upholds the benefits and possibilities of a life style of creative simplicity." Participants are also to develop ways by which congregations "can engage in a serious analysis of the systemic causes of current injustices and initiate action programs that will change them."

Development education as a specialized activity is well established in many countries. In Britain, the publication by the British Council of Churches of *World Poverty and British Responsibility* in 1967 as a Lenten study guide contributed to a now broadly based World Development Movement. Canadian churches have initiated a number of activities and have joined in others, including the annual Ten Days for Development campaign. In Canada and elsewhere, government funds are helping to underwrite development education efforts, including school curriculum materials. In many countries, individual denominations and ecumenical agencies have made development education an ongoing theme of Bible studies and church publications, curriculum and preaching materials. In some discussions, the term "development" is being overtaken by the concept of "liberation."

Through these various channels, prophetic voices are speaking out on world hunger and global injustice, military spending and human rights. The message is a sober one. "It is truly painful," Pope Paul told the World Food Conference, "to admit that, up to now, society seems incapable of tackling world hunger." And Dr. Philip Potter: "Development efforts so far have been powerless to redress the gap between the rich and the poor between and within countries." We need, said Dr. Potter, to move beyond "pious appeals for solidarity" to fresh understandings, radical actions and new models of development. Dr. Potter sees a mandate for "awakening the conscience of our people through preaching, teaching and example and thereby working for the mobilization of political will toward radical changes in the present international economic order. This includes taking steps to conscientize the rich everywhere to the need for a healthy reduction of their uncontrolled and suicidal consumer patterns and styles of life."

More and more individuals and groups are taking up the life-style challenge. Several hundred persons have signed the Shakertown Pledge since its formulation in 1974. The earliest signers, who had practiced

REMODELLING SUGGESTION

its principles all along, are now being joined by some for whom the Pledge means a real change. Signers declare themselves to be world citizens, committed to ecologically sound lives of creative simplicity and to sharing personal wealth with the world's poor. They are pledged to "reshaping institutions in order to bring about a more just global society in which each person has full access to the needed resources for physical, emotional, intellectual and spiritual growth." Others such as Bread for the World, the Friends, various U.S. Catholic bishops and local congregations are also urging voluntary reduction of individual consumption of meat, fertilizer and other scarce resources.

These various issues were also confronted at the Aspen Consultation on Global Justice, a meeting of American religious leaders in mid-1974. The gathering was convened by the Overseas Development Council, a private nonprofit organization which serves as a national focal point for discussion and research on issues related to development and public policy. At Aspen, discussions ranged widely over such topics as community education, life styles and personal witness, corporate responsibility and consumer action. The Consultation issued a Statement of Conscience by Christians and Jews which acknowledged that many current American national policies, institutional structures and "personal patterns of conduct and consumption are all inextricably linked to the ongoing and explosive global catastrophe of famine, hunger and malnutrition." The group affirmed a commitment "not merely to bring immediate relief to the suffering, but also to work toward the creation of global structures which will ensure basic dignity and humane existence for all people."

The World Council of Churches and its member churches have also been actively engaged in wide-ranging discussions of world hunger and development. (Some of its educational materials are listed in the section entitled "For Further Reference.") Its Central Committee in mid-1974 adopted "Threats to Survival," a statement viewing the world food crisis, along with wasteful consumption patterns, misuse of natural resources, war technology and the international economic system as a whole, as a major menace to the world's poor. From that perspective, some at the Council feel the World Food Conference failed to deal with the global crisis at its deepest roots. Looking beyond the Conference to the continuing threats to survival, the Council's statement observes that "The churches have a fundamental task for sustaining hope, rooted in conviction that God is yet working in his world to make all things new. . . . We believe that the crisis can and should be perceived by Christians as an occasion to participate more energetically in the radical transformation of human values and social realities."

In February, 1975 President Mikko Juva and the officers of the Executive Committee of the Lutheran World Federation issued "A Call for Personal and Corporate Sacrifice" on the part of its 92 member churches. The statement took particular note of the efforts of local churches in Asia, Africa and Latin America "to confront the issues of hunger, popula-

tion pressure, racial discrimination and violations of
human rights." It viewed "hunger, unjust structures,
exploitation, racial discrimination and comparatively
large military expenditures [as] a challenge to the
church's witness." The statement called on all
members to support "drastic changes in life style
patterns and systems... to overcome excessive consumption and waste in some places, excessive population growth in other places and overall maldistribu-
tion of economic goods... As Christians, we are
motivated by the biblical description of humanity as
one universal family of God's children."

The Church and Public Policy

Concern for more adequate programs to meet the
needs of the hungry on the one hand and deeper
understandings of the global imbalances which perpetuate hunger on the other lead naturally into the area
of public policy.

There are, of course, very real limitations on what
the churches and others can do to influence the
formulation of public policy. Some denominations
and individuals have theological reservations. Even
those who believe that religion should be concerned
about the governmental structures in which human
lives are set do not always know just where to begin.
And, when it comes to out-and-out lobbying, there
are severe constraints in many countries on what
non-profit agencies may do. In the U.S., for example,
they may not spend a substantial part of their funds
or staff time on lobbying efforts.

Nonetheless, there are useful ways of making views

about world hunger known. At the international level, some private agencies have consultative status at the UN, and a larger number are registered with the UN Office of Public Information, thereby receiving regular news of UN developments. "Non-governmental organizations" are now an established part of the UN scene, generally welcomed by UN officials and by most governmental delegations. Their presence at the World Food Conference communicated public concern about the issues to the delegates and was reflected in the substance and language of the resolutions adopted. They will also have a chance to make their views known at the first meeting of the new UN World Food Council in June, 1975 and at the UN Special Session on Development and International Economic Cooperation in September, 1975. The fourth session of the UN Conference on Trade and Development (UNCTAD IV), scheduled for mid-1976, provides another focal point for the influencing of international public policy.

In many individual countries, the implementation by national governments of the World Food Conference resolutions is a natural focus for the monitoring and influencing efforts of concerned individuals and groups. In Canada, broad coalitions of groups are working intensively at the provincial level, as is the Standing Committee on the Second Development Decade in Britain.

In the United States, the Graymoor Covenant pledges "to affect the policies of our national government by increasing legislative action through local networks and a strengthened voice in Washington."

The National Council of Churches itself has expressed a concern to define desirable public policies and to stimulate "appropriate government actions." Religious and other private agencies are credited with having helped in recent years to bring about a greater congressional emphasis on humanitarian and developmental assistance, a less political food aid program and a reversal of a House of Representatives vote in 1974 against U.S. participation in the World Bank's International Development Association. CWS and/or LWR have testified before congressional committees on four occasions in 1974 and once in early 1975 on such matters as grain reserves, food aid and follow-up to the World Food Conference. The Washington Interreligious Task Force on U.S. Food Policy (described in the following chapter) is a major channel for the legislative concerns of many Protestant churches, as is the U.S. Catholic Conference for the Catholic community.

Whatever the representation at the national level, there is no substitute for individual citizens writing their representatives to express general concern about world hunger or to support specific government actions. A number of college campuses are engaged in efforts in that direction. Bread for the World, a Christian citizen's movement on hunger and poverty founded in 1973, is seeking to organize local chapters in each U.S. congressional district. It has testified on several occasions before congressional committees and has recently launched Project 500 to train that many leaders for the legislative and educational task.

There is also need for churches and other con-

cerned groups to influence the economic policies and
practices of agribusiness and multinational corporations which directly affect the hungry. Until recently,
few religious or secular organizations have given much
thought either to the constructive contributions
which such corporations might make to alleviate
world hunger or to the negative effects which
corporate practices may already be having in poorer
nations. Chapter 6 provides the details of a new
attempt by U.S. churches to influence corporate
economic policies.

Governments concluded that the world food crisis
would not be solved in the absence of political will at
the national and international levels. The churches are
realizing that they can play a more imaginative and
constructive role in strengthening and shaping such
political will. They cannot make political decisions
for governments, of course, but they can influence
governmental actions. Informed religious voices in
national capitals and at the grass roots, when coordi-
nated with the churches' other efforts in program
outreach and education, can be an important source
of new hope for the hungry.

6

constructive actions

Various actions by governments, churches and other private groups and individuals are providing new hope for the hungry. Selected examples follow, drawn from a wide range of situations and locations, primarily from the private sector. They may suggest further action to concerned readers.

Norwegian Government Initiatives

Norway played a leadership role in the World Food Conference discussions. It viewed the world crisis in its broadest terms: "International economic and political structural conditions contribute to an unequal distribution of resources, including food....The only way of permanently solving this crisis is by means of general social and economic development, including more food production and better food distribution in developing countries." Norway advocated upgraded roles for women, breastfeeding as crucial to child nutrition, fish as a source of protein for human rather than animal and pet use and revised patterns of trade with developing nations. The world food system agreed upon at Rome benefits from two Norwegian contributions. The first is a gift of 10,000 tons of wheat per year for emergency needs, a modest amount to be sure, but a major commitment for Norway, which imports 90 percent of its wheat. To avoid having to make a 10,000 ton wheat purchase on the already tight world market, Norway will mix 10,000 tons of homegrown barely to stretch its reduced wheat imports for domestic consumption. Less barley available for cattle feed will reduce meat supplies and raise meat prices, thus moving Norwegian diets "towards a relatively lower consumption of grain-based animal products." The daily bread and meat of Norwegians thus becomes integrated into the new world food system. This leads to a second contribution: a concern for malnutrition in developed countries. After reviewing, at Norway's suggestion, developed country malnutrition among those who eat too much as well as among those who eat too little, the Conference underscored "the need for improving nutrition in all countries" and cautioned that "the present consumption patterns of the affluent need not be taken as a model."

Norway's pledges at the Conference were substantial: to increase development assistance, to contribute $7 million to a new UN fertilizer pool, to step up funds for research and nutritional education. Norway had already contributed $28 million to the UN Special Fund and had taken a leadership role in organizing the Fund's operation. On the home front, Norway has sought improved nutrition through education and consumer information, through food pricing policies to reduce the consumption of fats and sugar, and through legislation affecting food advertising.

The Sudan Follows up on the World Food Conference

The Sudan, Africa's largest country and one of the Most Seriously Affected group, also played an active role in the Conference. With only about 9 percent of the country's vast arable land under cultivation, the Sudan has yet to achieve agricultural self-sufficiency. In fact, malnutrition proliferated in 1973-74 under the hot breath of the drought from the Sahel to the West and Ethiopia and Kenya to the East. Looking past its own problems, however, the Sudan is hoping someday to become a breadbasket for its hungry continent.

"It is the declared policy of my government," the minister of agriculture told the Conference, "to involve the rural areas of the country in socio-economic development efforts by eliminating the problems of hunger, thirst, ignorance and disease." In the last four years with help from the governments of Britain, the U.S., Scandanavia, and elsewhere, more than 2.5 million new acres have been irrigated, with studies for an additional 12.5 million acres underway. The Sudan has also welcomed investment by agribusiness concerns and development projects by private groups. Through the Sudan Council of Churches, Christian agencies from all over the world (including Church World Service and Lutheran World Relief) have mounted a multi-million dollar development effort, largely in the Southern Region. The UN family of agencies is also active, particularly the UN Development Program, the Food and Agriculture Organization, UNICEF and (during the period following its civil war) the UN High Commission for Refugees. The World Bank in 1974 approved a $10.7 million agricultural development program which promises improved crops, livestock and nutrition for more than 60,000 farm families. Such a partnership in the interest of agricultural production among governments, bilateral and multilateral aid programs and business and private agency resources, was encouraged by the World Food Conference.

The Sudan government called a meeting in February, 1975 to design follow-up measures for the Sudan. The gathering dramatized for participants from various sectors the rich agricultural potential of the country. It is too early to anticipate what concrete measures may come out of the gathering, but it is widely regarded as having been a creative and timely initiative on the part of the Sudan Government of the sort which may set an example for the other developing nations to follow.

Canadian Citizen Action at the World Food Conference

By far the most effective lobbying effort by non-governmental organizations at the Conference came from a coalition of Canadian groups. The coalition is credited with having influenced the Canadian government to increase its food aid pledge substantially and may also have helped create a more receptive Canadian government attitude on matters of agricultural development and trade. Certainly it made Canadians at home more aware of the Conference issues.

The coalition had 13 observers in Rome, representing Canadian groups such as GATT-Fly (an ecumenical action group), the Catholic Organization for Development & Peace, the Council for International Cooperation, OXFAM, the United Nations Associations and the Hunger Foundation. In Canada, a network of contacts linked Ottawa to the five regions and their larger cities. Each day the team in Rome telephoned Conference news and analysis to Ottawa which then shared it through the network with local groups. These responded with cables to the Canadian delegation in Rome, letters to the Prime Minister and calls to members of Parliament. On one issue 250 cables were received in Rome, some of them before the Canadian press had reported the Canadian government position to which the cables took exception. The government was challenged in parliamentary debate in Ottawa to explain its actions in Rome. The Canadian government delegation met regularly with the team in Rome.

Conference follow-up is now taking place across Canada. In the breadbasket provinces of Alberta and Saskatchewan, 19 regional seminars are being held to help develop appropriate food and trade policies at the provincial level. The groups are laying the ground-work for even more effective efforts at the Fourth UN Conference on Trade and Development in 1976.

Citizen Pressure on the U.S. Government

The World Hunger Action Coalition was created by various secular and religious groups in early 1974 to bring U.S. citizen concern about world hunger to bear on government planning for the World Food

Conference. A Coalition-sponsored National Week of Concern for World Hunger in September was proclaimed by many governors and mayors and observed by countless citizens throughout the country. The Coalition presented the State Department with petitions urging U.S. leadership in the Conference discussions and pledging sacrificial action to combat starvation. The coalition disbanded shortly after the Conference, as planned.

UNCTAD Sunday, The Netherlands

On April 13, 1972 the Third UN Conference on Trade and Development (UNCTAD III) convened in Santiago, Chile to hammer out more equitable patterns of trade between developed and developing countries. April 11 was UNCTAD Sunday in Holland. The Dutch Council of Churches, in coordination with a coalition of about 150 action groups, put UNCTAD on everyone's map. A joint ecumenical service was carried on Dutch national radio and television. Catholics and Protestants joined in a new liturgy around the issue of world trade, sang newly written hymns, and delved into specially prepared educational materials. The World Council of Churches worked with the Dutch Council by suggesting ideas and putting planners in touch with similar ventures elsewhere. Policy recommendations were made to the Dutch government, and the meetings in Santiago were followed with great public interest. Life and death issues for developing countries such as tariffs and market access, primary commodities and trade preferences became household words in Holland.

Community Development in Haiti

The island of La Gonave lies in a bay just off the Haitian capital of Port-au-Prince. Like the country as a whole, its 55,000 people suffer from grinding poverty, chronic malnutrition and isolation from the outside world. Its 330 square miles are the poorest area of one of the world's hungriest countries, as the map in Chapter 1 indicates.

The Service Chretien d'Haiti (SCH) began an ambitious program of community development in 1971. Top priority was given to road construction projects to open up contact among 22 villages and with ports from which produce could be shipped to the Port-au-Prince market. Local committees in each community have planned and carried out the road-work under the guidance of SCH staff. Workers are paid in foodstuffs from the U.S. Food for Peace Program through Church World Service and with food contributed by U.S. farmers through CROP. SCH also provides tools and technical assistance as needed. After five years and tens of thousands of hours of work, a network of 57.3 miles of dirt roads now links the island's communities.

At the same time, other projects have been carried out, some also along food-for-work lines. A reforestation nursery has been set up which in 1973 sold farmers 12,000 seedlings at nominal prices. Its local staff of 30 maintains an inventory of 15,000 seedlings (including coffee, grapefruit and mahogany) and using a cooperative garden demonstrates new crops, new cultivation techniques, the use of compost and soil conservation methods such as dry-wall terracing. A cooperative farm now grows peanuts, a crop fairly new to the area. Springs have been capped and community water supplies improved, a school constructed, and a workshop begun to train men in carpentry and women in handcrafts. A fishing co-op to tap off-shore food resources is under discussion.

In 1972, SCH helped carry out the first census of the island's population. Then came a comprehensive vaccination program by government and private teams on foot and by jeep and boat. The United Methodist Committee for Overseas Relief through CWS provided most of the vaccine for the youngest children; from other sources came vaccine and innoculation equipment for older children, women, and men. By 1974 89 percent of the island's people have received an initial round of shots; the second round is about half complete. In the process, the serious cases of malnutrition discovered (a few in the coastal villages where fish is available, more in the interior) have been referred for treatment.

These projects over a five year stretch have made a significant difference in the lives of the people of La Gonave—although malnutrition has not been eradicated. The island's churches, which have grown closer in the process, have masterminded the effort assisted by church agencies from the United States, Germany and Canada.

Indonesian Planners at the Grass Roots

The development planners at the Development Centre of the Indonesian Council of Churches have

gone to remote villages to live with the people, find
out their priorities, learn about their daily problems
and listen to their planning-for-change at the local
level. For academicians from the capital, it was not
easy to accept the resources and potentials of the
local level as a basis for planning. Nor was it easy to
experience the life of the people at subsistence levels,
limited by cultural and feudalistic traditions, and still

Chic. ©Punch ROTHCO

*" She's got a point there—does she
take the pill before or after what
would have been a meal time?"*

to encourage them to design ways to improve their situation. What sort of plans will emerge from the experience, and whether assistance from outside churches will be requested, is not clear.

A Boost for Indian Farmers

The Baramati Project in the Maharashtra State of India has enabled subsistence farmers in 45 villages to create a network of reservoirs and wells to improve their erratic water supply. Like many in India, where more than half of the land depends for water solely on rainfall, their fate had fluctuated between drought and floods, between too little water and too much.

The Baramati Project grew out of the work of two career missionaries. Beginning in 1972, they worked with the villages to build dams which created ten artificial lakes, in turn making irrigation possible and raising the ground water level in the area. Villagers were paid for work on the dams at a rate of four pounds of grain and one pint of oil per day from food commodities provided by the U.S. government through CWS and LWR. LWR also made available to workers and their families blankets provided by Lutheran congregations in the U.S.

Full use of the ground water requires wells, irrigation pumps and other equipment. A Baramati Agricultural Development Trust has therefore been set up which provides farmers with loans of about $1,350 each, repayable over a period of seven years. A $67,500 grant by LWR to the Trust has been placed in an Indian bank to serve as collateral for the loans. Already the Trust has drilled more than 200 successful wells and the farmers are growing two crops instead of one and getting better yields. An Indian agency, Action for Food Production, has provided assistance to village advisory committees. The National Christian Council of India has welcomed the venture.

Community Hunger Appeal, U.S.A.

CROP is the Community Hunger Appeal of Church World Service (CWS). Through its network of national and regional offices, and its committees at the state, county and local levels, it seeks to help communities learn about world hunger and raise funds for CWS and other agencies. During 1974, a total of $5 million was raised, mostly in cash but also in clothing, blankets and other donated items, including boxcar loads of food crops from U.S. farmers.

Hunger walks have become an effective technique through which CROP helps Americans identify with people in developing countries who walk every day in search of food, water, and other necessities. U.S. walkers raise funds from sponsors who pledge a certain amount for each mile walked. A Walk for the Hungry on November 17, 1974 sponsored by the Pomona, California Council of Churches drew people of all ages from 50 churches, Catholic and Protestant. The 1,800 walkers earned a total of $29,319. CROP-sponsored hunger walks in 1974 involved 90,000 people and raised $1,521,000.

Another CROP technique has been a fast, involving 3,000 participants in about 100 communities in 1974. For about thirty hours, usually on week-ends, fasters forego food in order to get a sense, however fleeting, of what it feels like to be hungry. The fast-time is used for reflection and discussion of hunger at home and abroad, personal and corporate life styles, and institutional changes needed to bring hope for the hungry. Fasts often end with a Third World Banquet in which the group is arbitrarily divided into thirds. One third gets a typical U.S. meal, one third a refugee meal (such as is served by CARE or CWS overseas), and one third a serving of rice. This frequently leads to sharing of scarce food and to further reflection on the capriciousness of hunger.

A Local Congregation Acts

The Presbyterian Church in Blackshear, a tobacco-growing community of 3,000 in rural southeastern Georgia, has drawn world hunger into its everyday life. Through the efforts of the pastor and the church's Hunger Task Force, the congregation has studied the problem and acted. Using its denomination, the Presbyterian Church in the U.S., and Church World Service, it supports programs of relief and agricultural development in Honduras, Ghana, the Sahel, and Bangladesh. It now reaches out to publicize the federal foodstamp program among the hungry in its area. Recently it voted to use the offering from the first Sunday of each month for its hunger work.

The congregation, which numbers about 170, has also reached out to other churches and civic groups such as the Rotary Club. A joint hunger walk in 1974 earned $600; the 1975 target is $4,000. The high school has agreed to serve students soup one day each week, with the money saved from usual lunches to be used for hunger concerns. The Black shear delegates to the State Youth Assembly plan to place before the state legislature a bill on the subject of hunger. These common efforts have brought a new degree of closeness among the churches and within the community and have won praise from local government officials.

The pastor of the church, the Rev. Richard Bass, is one of the denomination's fourteen Hunger Action Enablers in about as many states. The enablers work with local presbyteries, over half of which now have their own Hunger Task Forces. The decision of the General Assembly of the Presbyterian Church in 1969 to make hunger a top priority concern has had a pervasive impact throughout its life and mission at every level.

Reflecting on the experience of his church, Mr. Bass says, "I think the focus and ministry of any church has to be worldwide. What happens in Bangladesh affects people in Blackshear. We are all part of one global community where isolationism is unthinkable. The church has a worldwide mission. We need to hear what people in other parts of the world are saying. The gospel is enriched by the participation and insights of people of the whole world."

Bennett v. Butz

Between 37-50 million Americans were eligible for federal food programs of one sort or another in 1974; only 17 million were enrolled. Persons qualify for food stamps who are on welfare or whose family-of-four net income is less than $513 per month. Food stamp benefits are related to family size and net income. A family of four having a net income of $300 per month must pay $83 for $154 in food stamps. In late 1974, the average participant in the program received a benefit of about $20 per month.

Rather than spend $278 million authorized by Congress for outreach to make millions of low-income people aware of the nutrition benefits due them by law, the Nixon administration decided to return that amount to the U.S. Treasury. In *Bennett v. Butz,* a federal district judge in Minnesota in October, 1974 ordered the U.S. Secretary of Agriculture Butz to spend the money, as intended, to expand the coverage of a program "designed to alleviate hunger and malnutrition by increasing the food purchasing power of low-income households."

The suit which forced the Department of Agriculture to spend funds to publicize the food stamp program was brought by three low income people and three law firms. One, the Food Research and Action Center (FRAC), is funded in part by Protestant, Catholic and ecumenical groups at the national and local levels. (Originally it received funds from OEO, the U.S. Office of Economic Opportunity.) FRAC is a non-profit, public interest law firm concerned exclusively with the elimination of hunger in America. It provides free legal assistance to poor people who are defending their rights under governmental food assistance programs. In addition, FRAC monitors the administration of such government programs, publishes handbooks on their operation, and provides community organizing assistance to community groups that are working to end hunger. It has encouraged and equipped local congregations to do their own outreach to the hungry and even to operate their own programs. FRAC has also provided staff services to the National Council of Churches' Crusade Against Hunger.

While *Bennett v. Butz* is the FRAC-related case which has had the widest national impact on hunger in America, the firm has helped to win a number of victories, including two in the U.S. Supreme Court, which have provided new hope for hungry migrants, Indians, Puerto Ricans, rural and urban poor. It has sued 17 states with the poorest outreach records to insure that state welfare departments use U.S. funds as directed by the *Bennett v. Butz* ruling.

The Churches and Agribusiness

"Should the church send missionaries to foreign countries to aid the poor and then invest to make money in American companies whose foreign policies exploit the people and insure the continuance of poverty?"

This question is asked by the Interfaith Center on Corporate Responsibility (ICCR), an ecumenical committee of religious groups owning stock in corporations and concerned about socially responsible investments. Among its members are 22 national church agencies in the U.S. and Canada, Protestant and Catholic, and the National Council of Churches. Its Task Force on Eco-justice is answering the question by reviewing the economic interconnections between agribusiness and world hunger. Out of its study and discussions have come a number of actions.

In November, 1974, an ICCR *Brief* treated "Agribusiness and Food Crisis". In early 1975, ICCR initiated dialogue with major U.S. fertilizer and grain companies to learn more about their policies and practices. A number of participating groups have joined in a stockholder resolution with the TENNECO Corporation, whose subsidiaries own more than a million acres of U.S. land and control large-scale food packaging, processing, marketing and distribution operations. Resolutions have been filed with Bristol-Myers and American Home Products, companies whose promotional appeals for infant formulas are alleged to contribute to malnutrition by discouraging breastfeeding in developing countries.

The results of ICCR activities in other fields such as South African investments and strip mining augur well for these new agribusiness efforts.

Washington Efforts on World Hunger

The Washington Interreligious Staff Council (WISC) in 1974 established a special Interreligious Task Force on U.S. Food Policy. The Task Force is composed of about 15 Washington-based professional staff of Protestant, Roman Catholic and Jewish national agencies who are responsible for U.S. food policy issues in their own organizations, and who have pledged to share and coordinate their efforts in order to increase their services to the American religious community. The sole concern of the Task

Force is to facilitate the development of a responsible U.S. food policy by monitoring government decisions and actions, by providing easy access to information, and by recommending guidelines for more just governmental policies.

The Task Force on U.S. Food Policy in late 1974 prepared and distributed a study, "Some Policy Options for Dealing with the World Food Crisis." It sees the 1975-76 congressional sessions as a time of

Claudius Ceccon. By permission of Claudius Ceccon and the World Council of Churches.

major rethinking of such critical matters as food aid, food stamps, and farm policy (including production, prices, fertilizer and grain reserves). Also high on the agenda are economic relationships with other nations and U.S. participation in the UN (including the World Food Council and the International Fund for Agricultural Development).

In order to disseminate information and stimulate concern, WISC has established IMPACT, an information and action network. IMPACT sends out mailings periodically on a wide range of federal legislative policy issues to more than 6,000 individuals who have pledged to be in touch with their legislative representatives at least three times per year. Since hunger is a special priority for WISC, an additional IMPACT/Hunger series of publications is planned for 1975-76.

The work of the Task Force on U.S. Food Policy and other task forces is facilitated by the Washington office of the National Council of Churches. Through a regular newsletter called MARK-UP, the Council keeps local, state and national councils of churches posted on legislative developments regarding hunger and other issues. It also publishes a regular summary of the *Congressional Record* with special attention to food policy items and works with denominations to arrange meetings with Washington officials for interested church groups.

These vignettes are meant to stimulate action, not to prescribe what forms it should take. (For those who find these sample actions intriguing, additional information, including addresses, is given in the section which follows.) The question, "What shall I do?"

is best left to each person and to each community.
Actions will be shaped by many factors, including
one's reading of the world food crisis, the context
and communities in which one's life is set, and the
responses which seem to make the most sense. Even
within the religious community, there will be wide
diversity of action according to the convictions and
styles of those involved. There is no blueprint for
personal or corporate action any more than for governmental response.

Nonetheless, it is clear that there are three major
action fronts to be considered by individuals and
groups: program outreach, education and life-style
patterns, and the influencing of political and economic policies. Actions will doubtless be the most
helpful which are part of a concerted strategy on one
or more of these three fronts. Actions should also
differentiate carefully between the emergency crisis
and the underlying global imbalances, between the
domestic and the international dimensions of the
problem, and between what governments and the
private sector can each do best. This does not mean
that one concentrates exclusively on the long term, or
the domestic scene, or the governmental response,
but rather that actions on one front keep the full picture in view.

While action by individuals is clearly necessary,
nothing short of joint action will begin to alter the
global imbalances which perpetuate hunger. The question, "What shall I do?" is less important, then, than
"What shall we do?" Yet even joint action of a given
sort is not a response sufficient unto itself.

The moderation of life styles, for example, by reducing grain consumption or fertilizer use in developed countries will fall short of the beneficial impact intended unless it is part of a more mult-faced effort which includes supporting constructive private and governmental efforts with the money and material thus saved and working to shape laws to assure the transfer of food and fertilizer to people in need. Calls on governments for increased food aid overseas and reduced fertilizer use on government property at home themselves become more convincing in the context of moderated food consumption by groups of private citizens and reduced fertilizer use on private and church property.

Similarly, vastly expanded relief and development programs through greater private contributions, imperative though they be, will surely fall short of meeting proliferating human needs unless governmental efforts themselves are at the same time expanded and refocused. Neither can do the job alone. And in the final analysis, all aid efforts, both public and private, essential though they be, are probably less crucial than revisions in the basic economic relationships between rich and poor countries and between the rich and poor within countries. An informed and politically active citizenry is doubtless more essential to the ultimate eradication of world hunger than a compassionate one.

Since the world food crisis is here to stay, concerned individuals should take time to learn about it in greater detail before moving into action. The final section of this book includes resources for

reading and study. There is surely continuing induce-
ment for such study, since our daily lives are caught
up directly in the crisis. "Agriculture," the saying
goes, "is as far away as your next meal." The world
food crisis, however, will not wait long for us to
understand it. Those who care must act promptly
along lines which they themselves choose to join with
those already seeking to provide new hope for the
hungry.

epilogue

There have been some encouraging developments in the month which has elapsed since I began to write this book. Pakistan reports an easing of her emergency food needs, thanks to almost $1 billion in aid from oil producing countries. That Most Seriously Affected nation now expects self-sufficiency in food production in two or three years as a large irrigation project and several fertilizer plants become operational. India and Bangladesh have almost arranged to purchase, on deferred payment terms, the last 500,000 tons of wheat each needs for this year's emergency. Russia has cancelled an order for 200,000 tons of U.S. wheat, China one of 600,000 tons. The UN's early warning system reports that "serious food shortages" in the Sahel have given way to less desperate "food shortages". The new World Food Council will soon have a secretary general and is working on the agenda for its first meeting. The United States has announced a food aid level of about 5.5 million tons, up 2.2 million from 1974. An excellent crop of U.S. winter wheat is forecast. A Ford administration proposal to raise food stamp costs to low-income people was rebuffed by Congress.

Most of these developments, encouraging at first glance, provide only modest hope for the hungry. India and Bangladesh may have mortgaged their futures to meet immediate food needs, since deferred payments must sooner or later be repaid. With lower world commercial demand and favorable crop predictions, some U.S. farm groups are urging farmers once again to retire cropland to avoid generating new "surpluses." (From the vantage point of a hungry world there are no surpluses.) The U.S. food aid decision comes so late in the year that the quantities approved probably cannot be shipped in time, and their political destinations seem more clear than their humanitarian ports of call. The U.S. Congress, while staving off a cutback, did not consider increasing the purchasing power of food stamps or the incomes of the poor. More ominously still, American fertilizer companies, faced with U.S. demand, are saying that, for the next several years, "We just don't have any fertilizer available for the foreign market." All of these events underscore the absence of a rational world food policy and of measures in the United States and elsewhere supportive of it. The news from Pakistan, the Sahel, and the World Food Council emerges as perhaps the most hopeful of the month.

In all fairness, a single month should not be expected to make a great deal of difference in the world food crisis. Improved weather, increased supply and decreased commercial demand are all welcome, but none of them change the global imbalances beneath the crisis any more than do food aid, petro-dollars and contraceptives. Altering those root imbalances is a matter of years and not months. These few positive but superficial changes have by no means reached the half billion people whose hunger is neither met automatically by increased food supply nor reflected in commercial food demand. The chronically hungry are still hungry.

Throughout this past month's writing, I have found myself haunted by the words of the Magnificat: "He has filled the hungry with good things, and the rich he hath sent empty away." A puzzling commentary on absolute poverty and proliferating malnutrition, indeed. Similarly enigmatic are the

remarks of Mother Theresa to the U.S. Senate Foreign Relations Committee about her work in Calcutta. "The poor are the hope of mankind and also the hope of the people of America. . . . The people of America need the poor. We will receive much more from them than we will give them." From these paradoxical perspectives, the solution of the world food crisis becomes an issue not of humanitarianism but of self-respect, not of supplementary feeding but of human survival, not of charity but of justice. We must make hope real in the very tangible forms of bread and justice. Refusing to respond fully to the challenge of the world food crisis may send us all empty away.

The last word belongs to the Zambian minister of rural development. He told the World Food Conference:

> Today man, man who has wrestled with nature and tamed it, man who has conquered disease, man who has silenced the tempestuous seas and summoned forth the other planets to admire his feats, faces the danger of the total extinction of his species at the hands of a formless, shapeless pestilence called hunger. The sand dunes of hunger stand in a brooding horrible vigil over parts of Latin America, Africa and Asia. Tomorrow these harbingers of destruction will shift, as sure as night follows day, into the honeyed territories of developed countries. . .As a human race we have only this one planet to share. As a people our destiny is only one—in the long run to live and prosper together or to perish together in a self-inflicted holocaust. Through the blessings of better communications the world is becoming more and more closely knit—it is becoming more and more one. We have yet time, time to make it one world for progress. We have little time to make the world one against hunger.

for further reference

United Nations Materials

The data on which this book is based was prepared by the **UN World Food Conference Secretariat** for the Conference. The essential documents are *The Assessment of the World Food Situation—Present and Future, Proposals for National and International Action* and *The Report of the World Food Conference.* The data in Chapters 1 and 2 is drawn primarily from the *Assessment;* in Chapters 3 and 4, from the *Action* and *Report* documents. All are available free of charge from the Center for Economic and Social Information (CESI), United Nations, New York, N.Y. 10017. Also available from CESI is the *Declaration of the Rome Forum on World Food Problems* mentioned in Chapter 4. The UNICEF material in Chapter 1 is drawn from "Facts Behind Emergency for Children" (June, 1974), available from **UNICEF,** United Nations, New York, N.Y. 10017. Chapters 1 and 4 draw data and quotations from the 1973 and 1974 "Addresses of the President to the Board of Governors of the **World Bank,**" available from the International Bank for Reconstruction and Development, 1818 H Street N.W., Washington, D. C. 20433.

The address of the UN Office of Public Information
(Chapter 5) is United Nations, New York, N.Y.
10017. The speeches of various delegates at the
Conference (Bangladesh in Chapter 1, Ireland, Cuba
and Tanzania in 2, Pakistan and Liberia in 3, New
Zealand and Argentina in 4 and Zambia in 4 and the
Epilogue), and from the Netherlands delegate to the
Special Session (Chapter 3) are available through the
New York or Washington missions of those countries
to the UN. The speech by Ambassador Scali to the
General Assembly (Chapter 4) is available from the
U.S. Mission to the UN, 799 UN Plaza, New York,
N.Y. 10017.

Other Materials

Quotations from Ambassador Martin (Chapter 3),
from the U.S. Senate Report (3), and from U.S.
Secretary of Agriculture Butz (4) are drawn from
1975 U.S. Agricultural Outlook, available from the
U.S. Senate Committee on Agriculture & Forestry,
U.S. Senate, Washington, D.C. 20002. The testimony
about Bangladesh (1) is part of an Ad Hoc Senate
Hearing on Follow-up to the World Food and
Population Conferences (December 18, 1974), available from the Senate Select Committee on Nutrition
and Human Needs, U.S. Senate, Washington, D.C.
20002. The remarks of Mother Theresa in the Epilogue
are reprinted in the Senate Foreign Relation Committee Report of Hearings held on June 6, 1974 on
Senate Resolution 329.

The excerpt in Chapter 1 by Ms. de Jesus is found
on page 152 of her book, *Child of the Dark,* the New
American Library, New York, N.Y. 1962, used by
permission of E. P. Dutton & Co., Inc. Ms. Jones'

story in Chapter 1 comes from a story by Harry B. Anderson in the *Wall Street Journal,* December 3, 1974. The experienced observer cited in Chapter 3 is Dr. C. Dean Freudenberger, **Bread for the World** observer at the WFC. His report on the World Food Conference appeared in the December, 1974 Bread for the World Newsletter, available from the National Office at 235 East 49th St., New York, N.Y. 10017.

Military expenditure figures in Chapter 4 are drawn from *Military Balance 1973-1974,* by the International Institute for Strategic Studies, London; "World Military Expenditures and Arms Trade, 1963-73," by the U.S. Arms Control and Disarmament Agency, "The Defense Monitor," a series published by the Private Center for Defense Information, 201 Massachusetts Ave. N.W., Washington, D.C. 20002; and *World Military and Social Expenditures 1974,* by Ms. R. L. Sivard, published by the Institute for World Order, 11 W. 42nd St., New York, N.Y. 10017. The quotation marks on chart 4 enclose information from "The Defense Monitor" of May, 1973. An analysis of the relationship between military and development expenditures is available from the World Conference for Religion and Peace, 777 UN Plaza, New York, N.Y. 10017.

Data and analyses on the impact of oil prices, trade, and public opinion on development (Chapter 2) are available in *Agenda for Action, 1974* and other publications of the **Overseas Development Council,** 1717 Massachusetts Ave. NW, Washington, D.C. 20036. More information on voluntary agencies (Chapter 5) is available from the **American Council of Voluntary Agencies,** 200 Park Ave. South, New York, N.Y. 10003. For an overview of agencies registered with the U.S. government, *A Look to the Future: The Role of Voluntary Agencies in International Assistance* is available from the Advisory Committee on Voluntary Foreign Aid, Agency for International Development, Washington, D.C. 20523. Each individual voluntary agency has its own publications. **Church World Service** is located at 475 Riverside Drive, New York, N.Y. 10027. **Lutheran World Relief** is at 315 Park Avenue South, New York, N.Y. 10015.

Dr. Potter's address to the World Food Conference (4 and 5), a pamphlet on the Ecumenical Development Cooperative Society, and packets of information on Development Education (5 and 6), People's Participation in Development (4), and Appropriate Technology (4) are available from the U.S. Office of the **World Council of Churches**, at 475 Riverside Drive, New York, N.Y. Room 439. The vignette from Indonesia and the technology cartoon in 6 are taken from such packets. The Lutheran statement of February, 1975 referred to in Chapter 5 is available from the USA National Committee of the **Lutheran World Federation** at 315 Park Avenue South, New York, N.Y. Pope Paul VI's address (3 and 5) is available from the Office of the Permanent Observer of the Holy See to the UN, 323 47th St., New York, N.Y. 10017.

The Graymoor Covenant and materials on hunger efforts by the National Council of Churches and its member denominations (Chapter 5) are available from the NCC Coordinator of Hunger Concerns, Room 626, 475 Riverside Drive, New York, N.Y. 10027. These efforts are also the subject of an article in the February 3, 1975 issue of *Christianity and Crisis*, a special issue devoted to world hunger. (The same issue includes "The U.S. and the World Food Conference" by the author.) The **Washington Inter-religious Task Force on World Hunger** (5 and 6), is located at 100 Maryland Ave. NE, Washington, D.C. 20002, (202) 543-1126. The National headquarters of **CROP** (5 and 6) is at P.O. Box 968 Elkhart, Indiana 46514. **The Food Research & Action Council** (6) is at 25 W. 43rd St., New York, N.Y. 10036. **The Shakertown Pledge Group** has offices at 4719 Cedar Avenue, Philadelphia, Pa. 19143. The material concerning the Blackshear, Georgia Presbyterian Church is adapted from an article by Ms. Carolyn Curtis in the *Presbyterian Survey* issue of March, 1975, and used by permission.

ADDITIONAL MATERIALS

A wide range of resources await the interested reader.* Among those which deal in greater detail with the themes of this volume are the following:

1. Brown, Lester R., *By Bread Alone*, New York: Praeger, (with E.P. Eckholm), 1974, $8.95 (paperback $3.95).
2. Fenton, Thomas P., *Education for Justice: A Resource Manual*, Maryknoll, New York: Orbis Books, 1975.
3. Gallis, Marion, *Trade for Justice: Myth or Man-*

---

*All Friendship Press publications listed are available through denominational bookstores and literature headquarters.

date? Geneva: World Council of Churches, 1972, $2.75.

4. Goulet, Denis, A New Moral Order: *Reflections on Development, Ethics and Liberation Theology*, Maryknoll, New York: Orbis Books, 1974.

5. Howe, James W., *The US & the Developing World: Agenda for Action, 1974,* New York: Praeger, 1974, $5.95 (paperback $1.95). 1975 edition available Spring, 1975.

6. Johnson, Byron L., *Need is Our Neighbor,* New York: Friendship Press, $1.75.

7. Kotz, Nick, *Let Them Eat Promises: The Politics of Hunger in America*, Englewood Cliffs, New Jersey, Prentice-Hall, 1969 (paperback: $1.95).

8. Lappe, Francis Moore, *Diet for a Small Planet*, Ballantine Books, New York, $1.50.

9. Myrdal, Gunnar, *The Challenge of World Poverty: A World Anti-Poverty Program in Outline*, New York: Pantheon, 1970.

10. Rountree, Estelle, and Halverstadt, Hugh (eds.), *Sometimes They Cry*, New York: Friendship Press, $3.50.

11. Simon, Paul and Arthur, *The Politics of World Hunger*, New York: Harper Press, 1973, $8.95

Audio-Visuals

1. *Crusade Against Hunger,* New York: Friendship Press, Color filmstrip, sound, $7.50.

2. *H-H Factor,* New York: Church World Service, color film; rental, $5.00; purchase, $30.00.

3. *Hungry World,* New York: Church World Service, color film; rental, $5.00; purchase, $20.00. (CWS materials available from 475 Riverside Dr., Room 656, New York, N.Y. 10027.)

4. *What's Nice? Rice!,* New York: Friendship Press, Color filmstrip, record, $7.50.